# Statesman and Saint

# Statesman and Saint

## THE PRINCIPLED POLITICS OF WILLIAM WILBERFORCE

## DAVID J. VAUGHAN

LEADERS IN ACTION
GENERAL EDITOR, GEORGE GRANT

HIGHLAND BOOKS

CUMBERLAND HOUSE • NASHVILLE, TENNESSEE

General Editor: George Grant

Published by
CUMBERLAND HOUSE PUBLISHING, INC.
431 Harding Industrial Drive
Nashville, Tennessee 37211
www.cumberlandhouse.com

Paperback Edition ISBN: 978-1-62045-392-6

**Library of Congress has cataloged the hardcover edition as follows**

Vaughan, David J., 1955–
    Statesman and saint : the principled politics of William Wilberforce / David J. Vaughan.
      p. cm. -- (Leaders in action series)
    Includes bibliographical references.
    ISBN 1-58182-224-3 (alk. paper)
      1. Wilberforce, William, 1759–1833. 2. Great Britain—Politics and government—1760–1820. 3. Great Britain—Politics and government—1820–1830. 4. Antislavery movements—Great Britain—History. 5. Philanthropists—Great Britain—Biography. 6. Abolitionists—Great Britain—Biography. 7. Legislators—Great Britain—Biography. I. Title. II. Series.

    DA522.W6 V38 2001
    326'.8'092--dc21
    [B]                                                      2001047704

*Printed in the United States of America*
1 2 3 4 5 6 7 8 9—05 04 03 02 01

*To my son Adam:*
*called to be a leader*

# CONTENTS

# FOREWORD

*William Wilberforce is that rarest of all breeds,*
*a man of great influence and station willing to*
*sacrifice all for the sake of truth. When we pray*
*that the Lord might be pleased to deliver us from*
*the hands of politicians and to entrust our future*
*to statesmen, we are unwittingly praying that*
*He would raise Wilberforce—and those few like*
*him—to ever higher positions.*[1]

                                        *—Thomas Chalmers*

*I*t has taken the perspective of twenty-twenty hindsight to see the extraordinary effects of William
Wilberforce's leadership. Though he was a remarkable
orator, though he was successful in assembling powerful
political, social, religious, and cultural coalitions, though
he was able to serve his nation ably and faithfully from
the time he was a young Turk to the time he was an
elder statesman, and though he was privileged to receive
the acclaim of friend and foe alike during his long career,
the fact is that the real effects of his leadership were not
readily evident in his lifetime. It is only by his legacy that
we are able to gauge his true impact on the men and
institutions of his time.

Like a latter-day Athanasius, Wilberforce stood *contra
mundum*, against the world. He was a contrarian in a day
of enforced conformity. He was a genuine reformer in a

day of sham revolutionaries. He was a man of unswerving principle in a day of latitudinarian compromise. At various times he was considered a fringe figure, a man who had squandered tremendous opportunities for the sake of his own stubbornness, and an uncompromising and single-minded fanatic. But it was precisely because he was willing to risk such stigmatization for the sake of justice and truth that he was able to prevail.

His contemporary, the great Scottish pastor, professor, and reformer Thomas Chalmers, likened him to George Washington, "who had the knack of losing every battle on his way to winning the war."[2] His tenacious and steadfast commitment to the cause of ending the African slave trade knew no moderation, accepted no defeat, and gave no credence to setbacks, mishaps, or obstacles. Likewise, Chalmers compared him to Admiral Nelson, "who gained the favor of immortal fame with his stunning victory at Trafalgar, but who had to pay the ultimate price for that favor: the whole of his life."[3] Wilberforce invested the whole of his life in his great cause, tasting victory only whilst upon his deathbed.

Thus, Wilberforce was a rather peculiar leader: one who was able to achieve his aims only after a lifetime of ardor.

That is hardly the sort of leadership we are likely to want to emulate these days. Our commitments tend to run toward slick contemporaniety, razzle-dazzle modernity, and gee-wiz fashionability. Indeed, we are afflicted by what Kenneth Meyers calls a "plague of terminal trendiness."[4] The result is that we have utterly lost what Steve Brown has called "old fashioned stick-to-it-iveness."[5] The difficult vocation of what Eugene Peterson has vividly dubbed "a long obedience in the same direction" is almost entirely missing from our lives and institutions.[6]

If for no other reason than that he has presented William Wilberforce as an anti-type to the modern leader, we owe David Vaughan a debt of gratitude. In *Statesman and Saint*, he has given us a glimpse of the very kind of leader we all actually long for, whether we realize it or not: a leader who stands for justice heedless of the cost; a leader unshaken by the exigencies of popular opinion, a leader willing to weather the firestorm of controversy that inevitably accompanies principled action, and a leader committed to a life of virtue and righteousness. Wilberforce was all that and more.

David Vaughan's historian's eye is everywhere evident in this little volume. But even more, his perspective as a pastor and community leader during difficult and challenging times is also obvious. That means that while the book shows all the careful literary craftsmanship and academic accuracy we might expect, it is supremely practical and remarkably inspirational as well. In other words, this is not just one more leadership profile; *Statesman and Saint* is, like its subject, that rarest of all surprises: solid, substantive, and stirring. With twenty-twenty hindsight, it shows us what leadership ought to be.

—George Grant

# Acknowledgments

T O ACCURATELY ACKNOWLEDGE ALL THOSE to whom I am indebted would require a separate volume. So I can only briefly mention a few of the friends and colleagues who continually encourage, support, and inspire me in my calling.

First of all, I am grateful to my wife and children. Diane has been, and continues to be, a selfless wife who gives away her husband to the many demands of ministry, writing, and speaking—without a word of complaint. She truly understands that we are "one flesh," and that any accomplishment or success of mine is equally hers. Indeed, without her, I would be laboring in vain. My children—Hannah, Lydia, Ethan, and Adam—miss their daddy when he is under the pressure of a deadline, but they know my love for each of them exceeds my interest in any project I may happen to be working on.

Special thanks are due to my staff: Tim and Kim Ward, Dave and Katherine Volz, Marty and Tammy Kinsey, Jim and Sue Hancock, Bryan and Debbie Short, and Jim and Cathy Cummings. I am also grateful to the board and staff of Liberty Classical School: Steve Griggs, the headmaster, and Denis Boyle, Sean McCartney, Mona Maynard (also my secretary), Nancy McCart, and

Mike and Andrea Bond. These are just some of the "saints" who labor with me for the good of our fellow man and the glory of God.

I am likewise indebted to Mike Macarty of KSIV radio for his example of public service and for the opportunity to reach the public through the Encounter program; to Jim Day of the St. Louis *MetroVoice* newspaper for his humor and for the space to ramble in print; and to Debi Fry of Liberty Networking for encouraging me and for providing a platform to address audiences nationwide.

Writing for Cumberland House is an author's dream come true. Ron Pitkin, the publisher, knows a good idea when he hears it, and is willing to venture where other publishers fear to tread. George Grant, the editor of the Leaders in Action series, is more than a colleague; he is a dear and respected friend who has done more for me than he will ever know.

Last, I must thank the Giver of all good gifts, who has abundantly blessed me with family, friends, and fellowship. My prayer is that he will condescend to use this book as an instrument to honor the memory of his servant William Wilberforce and to raise up a host of reformers who labor in his spirit.

# Introduction

*I*N THE BRITISH PORT CITY OF HULL stands the house where William Wilberforce was born. It is a large Jacobean red-brick house with great Georgian windows to let in the sunlight. Built in 1580 for the mayor of Hull, it passed into the Wilberforce family in 1732. It is now the Wilberforce House Museum.

In the front courtyard of the house stands a statue of William Wilberforce. In one of the rooms there are exhibits of the brutal instruments of slavery: branding irons, whips, shackles, slave collars, and thumbscrews. There are posters advertising slaves for sale. There is a receipt for one "Quamina," a good slave with bad legs.

Entering the adjoining room, one is startled by a small lifelike figure in dark clothes seated at a desk. This effigy of Wilberforce sits under two portraits, one of Thomas Clarkson and the other of Wilberforce himself, the two men who devoted their lives to abolition.

Within the room where Wilberforce was born is an inscription that summarizes his life and work:

> STATESMAN, ORATOR, PHILANTHROPIST, SAINT;
> ONE OF THE GREATEST PARLIAMENTARIANS IN A GREAT
> AGE, A FRIEND OF PITT AND BURKE, OF FOX AND
> CANNING—HE DID MORE THAN ANY OTHER MAN, BY

HIS ELOQUENCE AND COURAGE, HIS INDUSTRY AND PER-
TINACITY, TO BRING ABOUT THE ABOLITION OF SLAVERY
THROUGHOUT THE BRITISH EMPIRE. NO ENGLISHMAN
HAS EVER DONE MORE TO EVOKE THE CONSCIENCE OF THE
BRITISH PEOPLE AND TO ELEVATE AND ENNOBLE BRITISH
PUBLIC LIFE.

Wilberforce was a Statesman. As we will see, he was a man who put principle above party or personal interest, and who exercised political power for the benefit of the governed. It was once said that if Wilberforce had been willing to put party above humanity he could have become the prime minister of Great Britain. This is probably true. However, Wilberforce would not become a political prostitute in order to gain office or power. He was not a mere politician; he was a statesman.

Wilberforce was an Orator. Like other great statesmen of his day, he mastered the art of rhetoric and used his tongue as a trumpet of righteousness. He employed the power of the spoken word to speak for those who had no voice and who were suffering in silence. He boldly spoke the truth, even when opposed. He bravely pleaded for justice, even when ridiculed. Having received a divine commission, his oratory was an act of obedience to God. His consecrated tongue was a divine weapon.

Wilberforce was a Philanthropist. The story of his life is in some ways a story of the power of love. He had many virtues, but his kindness and benevolence permeated all his causes. His personal charm, which is legendary, shows the positive power of biblical charity—love for God and man. It is remarkable to see what one man may accomplish when filled with the spirit of love.

Wilberforce was a Saint. The term "saint" speaks of his explicitly Christian convictions, as well as his truly Christian character. Wilberforce did not hold a privatized faith; he did not divorce his Christianity from his long political career in the Commons. He was an unabashed evangelical Christian, and made no apologies for being so. But he was also a true Christian in private. And his noble character was a product of his genuine spirituality.

Speaking of saintliness, some readers may accuse me of writing hagiography rather than biography. They will find it hard to believe that a mere mortal could reach such heights of moral perfection, or that one man could accomplish so much good in his lifetime. They will charge me with drawing a caricature rather than a portrait. But it is not so, and I have even made a point of highlighting Wilberforce's faults. Yet when they are viewed next to his virtues, they pale in comparison.

Statesman, Orator, Philanthropist, Saint—reading the life of Wilberforce you will see that he was each of these—and more.

# CHRONOLOGY

1759 – Wilberforce born at Hull on August 4.
1766 – Wilberforce sent to Hull Grammar School where he is taught
        by Joseph and Isaac Milner.
1768 – His father, Robert, dies.
        Wilberforce is sent to live with Uncle William at Wimbledon
        where he is first exposed to Methodism. Educated at
        Putney.
1771 – Mother sends Wilberforce to Pocklington School; writes
        essays on "Friendship," "Popularity," and "Patience."
1776 – Attends St. John's College, Cambridge; meets William Pitt
        and Thomas Gisborne.
1777 – Uncle William dies, leaving Wilberforce an inheritance.
1780 – Wilberforce elected to Commons for Hull on September 11.
1781 – First speech in Commons on May 17.
1783 – Wilberforce, Pitt, and Eliot visit France in September and
        October; meet Marie Antoinette, Benjamin Franklin, and
        Marquis de la Fayette.
        On December 19, Pitt becomes First Lord of the Treasury.
1784 – March 25: Wilberforce makes famous Castle Yard speech.
        On April 1 reelected for Hull; on April 6 elected for Yorkshire
        County.
        In October Wilberforce sets off for continental tour (through
        February 1785) with Isaac Milner and family members;
        reads Doddridge's *Rise and Progress;* beginning of
        conversion.
1785 – In autumn Wilberforce takes second tour with Milner; read
        Greek New Testament together.
        November 24: Wilberforce writes to Pitt explaining conversion.

December 2: Wilberforce contacts Rev. John Newton;
    receives Pitt's reply.

1786 – Summer: Impeachment trial of Warren Hastings.

    Winter: Wilberforce is busy organizing the Proclamation
        Society.

1787 – Spring: Wilberforce lobbied by Clarkson to take up abolition.

    May: Establishment of Committee for the Abolition of the
        Slave Trade.

    June 1: Royal Proclamation for Encouragement of Piety and
        Virtue.

    November: Society to enforce the king's proclamation.

1788 – January: Wilberforce falls seriously ill.

    February 11: King directs a Committee of Privy Council to
        investigate the trade.

    May 8: Pitt proposes abolition should be debated in the next
        session of Parliament.

    June: Dolben's Bill passes, limiting the number of slaves
        carried on British vessels.

    October: Regency Crisis (Madness of King George until
        February '89).

    December 9: Wilberforce returns to Parliament after illness;
        on committee to examine royal physicians.

1789 – April: Privy Council inquiry finished.

    May 12: Debate on abolition. Wilberforce's first speech
        against the slave trade.

    July 14: Storming of the Bastille in Paris.

1790 – February: St. Georges Bay Company founded (later Sierra
        Leone Company).

    June: Wilberforce to Yorkshire for reelection; unopposed.

1791 – April 18: Wilberforce moves abolition of slave trade; defeated
        on April 20.

    Summer: Committee for Abolition produces one-volume
        abridgment of evidence for distribution to network of
        local assemblies.

    August 22: Slave uprising in San Domingo (St. Dominique).

1792 – Winter: News of San Domingo reaches England.

    April 2: Wilberforce moves for abolition of slave trade;

Dundas amendment carried.
1793 – January 21: Execution of Louis XVI.
February 1: France declares war on Britain.
February 22: Wilberforce moves again for abolition; again defeated.
Wilberforce introduces bill to abolish slave trade with foreign colonies; defeated.
August: Wilberforce begins draft of *Practical View*.
1794 – Wilberforce moves amendment for peace with France.
1795 – October: The radical London Corresponding Society meets and virtually calls for civil war.
November 10: Bills against treasonable practices and seditious meetings.
November 30: Opponents of bill gather at Castle Yard in York. Wilberforce arrives and gives speech for Loyalists, 7,000 of whom sign loyal petition.
1796 – February 18: Wilberforce moves for abolition. Defeated 74–70 on March 3.
June 7: Wilberforce reelected for York.
Summer: Busy with raising contributions for distressed, building more churches, reforming of hospitals.
December 21: Society for Bettering the Condition of the Poor.
1797 – February 14: *Practical View* ready for printer.
April: Publication of *Practical View*. Begins courtship of Barbara Spooner.
April 15: Navy mutiny at Spitland.
May 15: Wilberforce moves for abolition: defeated 82–74.
May 30: Wilberforce marries Barbara Spooner.
June: Trial of Thomas Williams, bookseller, for publishing Thomas Paine's *Age of Reason*.
June 12: Naval mutiny at the Nore.
1798 – April 3: Wilberforce again moves for abolition; again defeated, 87–83.
May 27: Duel between Pitt and George Tierney.
June: Wilberforce settles at Broomfield. Receives news of mother's death.
July 21: Birth of eldest son, William.

December 21: House debates bill to continue Habeas Corpus Suspension Act. Debate and investigation of prison at Cold Bath Fields.

1799 – Spring: Abolition again debated; defeated 84–54. Slave-carrying Bill and Slave Limitation Bill pass Commons but defeated in Lords, 27–32 (July 5).

April 12: Formation of Church Missionary Society.

June 18: Combination Act passed. Royal assent in July.

July 21: Birth of first daughter, Barbara.

1800 – February 17: Speech in favor of government rejecting Napoleon's peace offer.

October 18: Birth of second daughter, Elizabeth.

1801 – March 15: Pitt resigns; Addington appointed prime minister.

1802 – March 25: Peace of Amiens.

December 19: Birth of second son, Robert Isaac.

1803 – May 17: Renewal of war with France.

1804 – March 7: Foundation of the British and Foreign Bible Society.

May 7: Resignation of Addington; Pitt in office.

May 20: Wilberforce moves abolition of slave trade; carries by 124–49. Bill postponed in Lords until next year.

Summer: Brougham and Macaulay elected to Committee on Abolition.

1805 – February: Committee of Navy Inquiry presents report indicting Lord Melville for negligence.

April 8: Debate in Commons; Melville censored; impeachment fails.

September 7: Birth of third son, Samuel.

November: News of victory at Trafalgar.

December: News of defeat at Austerlitz.

1806 – January 23: Death of Pitt; Lord Henry Petty, Chancellor of the Exchequer.

March 31: Bill introduced to forbid the trade with any captured colony or foreign power.

May 18: Bill passes both Houses. General Resolution for abolition entered in both Houses. Final bill forbidding any new ship from entering trade. All the above measures carried with ease.

June: Fox becomes gravely ill; dies during the summer.

End of Summer Session: Wilberforce writes tract entitled *A Letter on the Abolition of the Slave Trade, etc.*

1807 – February 4: Abolition passes in Lords, 72–28.

February 23: Debate in House on abolition; passes 283–16.

March 25: Abolition receives royal assent.

June 5: Wilberforce reelected for Yorkshire.

September 22: Birth of youngest son, Henry William.

1808 – Wilberforce leaves Clapham (Broomsfield) and moves to Kensington Gore.

1809 – Scandal concerning duke of York.

1811 – February 5: Regency Bill passed.

May: Bill passed making slave trading a felony.

1812 – June: America declares war on Britain.

1813 – March 22: Debate on East India Company's charter.

1815 – February 8: Congress of Vienna; powers agree on declaration condemning slave trade.

March 1: Napoleon again seizes power in France.

March 29: Napoleon abolishes the slave trade in France.

May: Debate over Corn Laws.

June: Treaty of Vienna.

July 5: Registration Bill introduced in Commons; bill dies.

1816 – [The Black years—1816–1820—disastrous harvests.]

July 29: Meeting of Relief Society.

November 15: Riot at Spa Fields.

1817 – January: Prince Regent's coach assaulted; Wilberforce on secret committee to investigate.

June: "Oliver scandal."

1818 – August 16: St. Peter's Field Massacre—"Peterloo."

1820 – January 29: Death of George III; accession of George IV.

August: Trial of Queen Caroline.

1821 – May 24: Wilberforce offers leadership of the Anti-Slavery Campaign to T. F. Buxton.

July: George IV crowned.

December 30: Death of daughter Barbara.

1822 – January: Society for Abolition of Slavery (Emancipation).

1823 – May 15: Buxton makes motion in Commons for Emancipation.
　　　　August 18: Slave revolt in Demerara: John Smith, a Non-
　　　　　　conformist missionary, court-martialed (framed).
1824 – March 23: Wilberforce dangerously ill with inflammation of
　　　　　　the lungs.
　　　　June: Foundation of the Royal Society of the Prevention of
　　　　　　Cruelty to Animals.
　　　　June 11: Debate on missionary Smith.
　　　　June 15: Wilberforce's last speech in Parliament (just shy of
　　　　　　65th birthday).
1825 – Wilberforce moves from London; sells Kensington Gore.
　　　　February 22: Wilberforce retires from Parliament.
1826 – June 15: Wilberforce settles in Highwood.
1828 – Conflict with Vicar Williams over chapel built by
　　　　　　Wilberforce; beginning of son William's financial
　　　　　　problems.
1830 – May 15: Last appearance of Wilberforce in the chair of the
　　　　　　Anti-Slavery Society.
　　　　June 26: Death of George IV; accession of William IV.
　　　　November: Son William goes abroad to avoid creditors.
　　　　　　Wilberforce forced to move from Highwood Hill.
1832 – February: Daughter Elizabeth falls ill; dies on April 7.
　　　　June 4: Passage of Reform Bill.
　　　　Autumn: Wilberforce visits Clapham; sits for portrait by
　　　　　　Richmond.
1833 – April 12: Last public speech at Maidstone.
　　　　July 8: Abolition (Emancipation) Bill delivered by
　　　　　　government to West Indian agents.
　　　　July 25: Young Gladstone (future prime minister) has
　　　　　　breakfast with Wilberforce.
　　　　July 26: Third reading of Abolition of Slavery Bill passes
　　　　　　Commons.
　　　　July 29: Wilberforce dies.
　　　　August 5: Burial in Westminster.
1834 – Statue of Wilberforce erected in North Aisle of Westminster
　　　　　　Abbey.

# Statesman
# and Saint

# PART I
## THE LIFE OF WILLIAM WILBERFORCE

*Biography must be parsimonious of her honours; yet, even in the age of Burke and Mirabeau, of Napoleon and Wellington, of Goethe and of Walter Scott, she could not have justly refused them to one who, by paths till then untrodden, reached a social and political eminence never before attained by any man unaided by place, by party, or by the sword.*[1]

*It is the fashion of some contemporary historians to minimize the significance of moral factors in history; to conclude that regardless of such men as Woolman and Wilberforce, Livingstone and Lincoln, slavery would have disappeared anyway; and, indeed, that the errors of each generation of the past have been inexorably outmoded by the impersonal working of material forces. Such thinking is the vestigial remnant of a romanticism now sadly discredited.*[2]

*I thank the gods that I live in the age of Wilberforce and that I know one man at least who is both moral and entertaining.*[3]

# PROLOGUE

*S*LAVERY IS NEARLY AS OLD AS MANKIND ITSELF, its origin lost in the dark recesses of human history. Since brother rose up against brother, men have been at war with one another: murder and rapine, oppression and slavery, being the sorrowful staples of human history.

In the ancient world human slavery was widely practiced and cruelly condoned. Babylon, Egypt, Israel, indeed, all of the ancient empires were built upon the backs of slaves. Even the enlightened pagan philosopher Aristotle argued that slavery was part of the natural order; and Plato concurred, the working class of his ideal republic providing labor for the leisurely contemplation of the philosopher-kings. When Christianity dawned on the ancient West, there were so many slaves in the city that when it was proposed that they be designated by special dress, the idea was jettisoned for fear that the slaves would thereby recognize the strength of their numbers.[4]

Christianity, however, introduced a new ethic, indeed, a new worldview, which was subversive of the old regime of slavery. Now men*—all men—were seen as the handiwork of God, created in his image and equal before his throne. All men were the objects of his superintending providence and his sacrificial love. All men were included in his comprehensive call to salvation: "Whosoever thirsts may come and drink of the rivers of life freely."[5]

It is true that neither Christ nor his apostles forbade slavery (a fact that anti-abolitionists of a later day were quick to point out). Yet the teaching of the New Testament set the "peculiar institution" on a new footing. Yes, servants and slaves were told to be submissive to their masters; but now they were "free-men in the Lord." Their human dignity no longer depended on their social standing. Masters, too, were reminded to treat their slaves as fellow children of God, and to remember that they also had a Master in heaven to whom they would one day give account.

Teachings such as these could not but undermine the old pagan justifications for slavery. That is, of course, exactly what happened. As the gospel spread throughout Europe, the nations were discipled and the "heathen" bowed at the foot of the cross. In the West, the birth of Christendom meant the death of slavery. As Sir Coupland has noted:

> With the advance of civilization, Slavery slowly declined. In Europe the cessation of Roman con-

---

*I use the words *men* and *mankind* in the traditional sense of "all persons" regardless of gender or age.

*quest diminished the supply of slaves, and the*
*spread of Christianity, though it countenanced their*
*ownership, tended to improve their treatment and*
*raise their status. Gang-slavery for public works or*
*on big agricultural estates disappeared. Domestic*
*Slavery was gradually transformed into the looser*
*bondage of serfdom or villeinage, and so proceeded*
*. . . towards complete emancipation.*[6]

It was not until the age of exploration that slavery again unleashed its cruel whip. As Dutch, Spanish, and Portuguese merchants sailed to China, they had to round the forbidding obstacle of the Dark Continent. Trading posts were established on the west coast of Africa by the Portuguese and Spanish as the Dutch built a harbor in the southern extreme. While trafficking with the natives for gold, ivory, and pepper, their original object was to circumnavigate Africa in their quest for Asian and Indian riches. In 1444, however, the first shipment of "black gold" was sent to Lisbon and sold on the auction blocks. Thereafter, a regular trade evolved. Approximately five hundred slaves a year were sent from Africa to Portugal.

This moderate revival of slaving might never have blossomed had it not been for the discovery of the Americas. The promised wealth of the New World could only be realized with labor. Land was in plenty, and many riches buried in the earth, yet it had to be harvested. Who would provide the labor? The Indians of North America were too wild and free to be "seasoned" for slavery, and the Indians of the South had been decimated by sickness and sword. So Europe looked to Africa.

In 1515 the Portuguese began direct shipments to America, and in 1562 the famous buccaneer Sir John Hawkins shipped three hundred Africans to St. Domingo. When Queen Elizabeth heard of it she was horrified and warned him that any further trading in slaves would "call down the vengeance of Heaven on the undertakers."[7] There was, thereafter, little English slave trading until 1663 when the African Company was given a new charter that granted it a monopoly of the trade. The trade flourished, and the English built forts on the Gold Coast from which to harvest slaves. In 1713, through a treaty with Spain, England gained the *Asiento,* or sole right to supply the Spanish colonies with slaves. England was now officially in the slave business, and it was viewed as an integral part of British commercial and naval success. By the mid-eighteenth century, England became the leader of the trade—a dubious honor indeed.

Despite its mercantile advantages, the trade did not go unchallenged. The Nonconformist divine Richard Baxter criticized it, as did the poet Alexander Pope. The philosopher of the Glorious Revolution, John Locke, denounced slavery in his first treatise on civil government. In 1766 Bishop Warburton railed against slavery from his pulpit, claiming that "the infamous traffic for slaves directly infringes both divine and human law."[8] John Wesley in 1774 issued his widely read tract *Thoughts upon Slavery.* The ever-satirical Dr. Johnson greeted the publication of the American Declaration of Independence with the question "How is it that we hear the loudest yelps for liberty among the drivers of negroes?"[9] Politicians such as Burke and Walpole denounced it in Parliament. Poets such as Cowper and Southey derided it in letters. Divines such as Paley and Porteus damned it from their pulpits. Nevertheless, the trade prospered. Its poison had so infected the vital organs of English commerce that a cure was feared fatal to the patient.

A man was needed—a rare man—who could unite the disparate voices of protest and galvanize the nation to action. And not just any man but a politician: a man who had entrance to the halls of power and could use that power to break the stranglehold of plutocratic oppression. As Sir Reginald Coupland has pointed out, this man would have to possess a multitude of exceptional gifts.

> *He must possess, in the first place, the virtues of a fanatic without his vices. He must be palpably single-minded and unselfseeking. He must be strong enough to face opposition and ridicule, staunch enough to endure obstruction and delay. In season and out of season, he must thrust his cause on Parliament's attention. . . . Somehow or other he must be persistent, yet not unpopular. Secondly, he must possess the intellectual power to grasp an intricate subject, the clarity of mind to deal with a great mass of detailed evidence, the eloquence to expound it lucidly and effectively. He must be able to speak from the same brief a score of times without surfeiting his audience with a hash of stale meat. And, since the Slave Trade is his theme, he must have a certain natural delicacy of feeling. He will have terrible things to say; they will form an essential part of his case; but in the choice of them and in the*

> manner in which he says them he must avoid the
> besetting sin of the professional humanitarian. He
> must never be morbid. He must not seem to take a
> pleasure in dwelling on the unsavoury vices of his
> fellow men. He must not pile up the horrors and
> revel in atrocious details. He must shock, but not
> nauseate, the imagination of his hearers. Finally, he
> must be a man of recognised position in society and
> politics. . . . And he must have, or by some means
> obtain, a footing in Downing Street. For without at
> least some shadow of support from Government his
> task might well prove desperate.[10]

Who was this Herculean hybrid of passion and perseverance, selflessness and single-mindedness, ability and
access? You are about to meet him.

# EARLY YEARS, IDLE YEARS

*T*HE CITY OF HULL was the fourth largest port of England, ranking behind only London, Bristol, and Liverpool. At the convergence of two rivers, the Hull and the Humber, it was a prosperous port that derived its wealth from the Baltic trade. Timber came in from Norway, iron from Sweden, wood from Russia, and tobacco and rice from America. Later in the eighteenth century, it became a major whaling port, driving the upper classes out into the country during the summer when the stench of whale oil became insufferable. But Hull was more than a commercial port; it was also a center of "gay"* social life. Its many prosperous merchant families made Hull "the Dublin of England" for all its "hospitality" and "plenty of good cheer."[11]

---

*The word *gay* is used in the traditional sense of "cheerfulness," "merry," or "lighthearted."

It was here that William Wilberforce was born. His father, Robert, was descended from the first Wilberforce who moved to Hull. Also named William, Robert's father was born in 1690 and built the family fortune in trading. He was twice mayor of Hull, being elected the second time in 1745. The elder William dominated the Wilberforce clan in Hull, and regaled them with his personal reminiscences of the duke of Marlborough's battles and the Young Pretender's invasion. Grandfather William had two sons and two daughters. His eldest son (another William) married Hannah Thornton, whose father was a great Russian merchant and director of the Bank of England, as well as a member of Parliament. The younger son, Robert, married Elizabeth Bird of London, who gave birth to William Wilberforce (our subject) on August 4, 1759.

William was the only son of four children; two of his sisters died in their nonage. Indeed, William himself was so frail as a child that it is a providential wonder that he survived. His frame was feeble, his eyes weak, and his stature small. If he had been born during Classical times, he later reflected, he would most certainly have been abandoned to the dogs. Despite his handicaps, William was gifted with a keen, vigorous mind and a kind, affectionate nature.

In 1766, at the age of seven, William was sent to Hull Grammar School, where he had the good fortune to sit under the shadow of the Milner brothers. The elder brother, Joseph, was later to become famous for his monumental *History of the Church of Christ,* while the younger brother, Isaac, would excel as a mathematician and cleric. It was Isaac who was to have such a profound impact on William's life in the near future. Even at this early age, William's melodious voice was conspicuous. Milner used to place little "Billy" on a table so he could read to the other boys; thus he served as a model of elocution.

When Robert Wilberforce died two years later, young William was sent to live with his uncle William and aunt Hannah, who lived in London at St. James's Place and who owned a villa in Wimbledon. He attended a boarding school in Putney, which was, he later said, very different from his previous school; it was a place where they taught "everything and nothing" to young merchant boys. His experience there was not good. "I was sent at first amongst the lodgers and I can remember even now the nauseous food with which we were supplied, and which I could not eat without sickness." Overall, it was "a most wretched little place."[12]

Holidays, however, were a different matter. William loved and revered his aunt and uncle. And it was they who introduced him to real Christianity. Both were friends of the famous "Methodist" evangelist George Whitefield, the man most responsible for the Great Awakening in England and America. Whitefield, it so happens, had converted John Thornton, Hannah's brother, to Christ. Thornton, a great evangelical layman, was one of the most generous men of his day; and it was his estate at Clapham that later became "the Saints'" haven. Though it is uncertain whether young William ever heard Whitefield preach, he did sit under the ministry of John Newton, the parson of Olney in Buckinghamshire. Newton often

preached in London, and William and Hannah Wilberforce took young Wilberforce to hear the famous hymn-
writer and ex-slaver. As young William sat in church
enthralled by his sermons, he grew to reverence Newton
"as a parent."[13] The sermons of Newton and the exhortations of William and Hannah were turning "little Billy"
into a "Methodist."

But Wilberforce's mother would have none of it.
Alerted by the increasingly religious nature of his letters
home, Elizabeth rushed to Wimbledon to rescue her
son from the dangers of "enthusiasm."[14] Though she
herself attended the Established Church, Elizabeth was
not about to have her son become a religious fanatic.
She hurried her coach to the Wilberforces' with mater-
nal instincts blazing, rebuffed Hannah's pleas not to
deprive William of religious influence, and rushed him
home to worldly Hull. The departure was very painful
for him. "I loved them as parents," he later said of his
aunt and uncle; "indeed I was almost broken-hearted at
the separation."[15]

With William safely back in Hull, his mother strove
to scrub his soul of Methodism. When on holidays from
his new school in Pocklington, he was immersed in the
ways of the world. His family and friends tried to dispel
his religious spirit. He was taken to concerts and the theater and taught to play cards. He dined with the fashionable gentry of Hull at two, drank tea at six, played cards
until nine, and then consumed a great supper.

> *The theatre, balls, great suppers and card parties*
> *were the delight of the principal families of the*

*town. This mode of life was at first distressing to
me, but by degrees I acquired a relish for it, and
became as thoughtless as the rest. I was everywhere
invited and caressed. The religious impressions
which I had gained at Wimbledon continued for
a considerable time after my return to Hull, but
my friends spared no pains to stifle them. I might
almost say that no pious parent ever laboured more
to impress a beloved child with sentiments of piety,
than they did to give me a taste for the world and
its diversions.*[16]

The rounds of worldly gaiety continued for five
years until William went up to Cambridge and entered
St. John's College in October of 1776. The alma mater
of such notables as Wyatt, Ascham, Fairfax, and Still-
ingfleet, St. John's was for Wilberforce another temptation to continue a life of harmless hedonism. Some of
the more licentious students drank hard and were vulgar
in speech and conduct. Others, like Wilberforce, were
merely social dilettantes who wasted their time in sober
dissipation. The object of his fellow students, said Wilberforce, was to "make and keep me idle."[17] Apparently,
they succeeded. His natural love for the classics led him
to read more than he might have otherwise; yet, for the
most part, he neglected his studies, seldom attended lec-
tures, and spent the majority of his time at card parties
and idle amusements. All of this was congenial to his
affable nature, of course. He was naturally witty, charming, and sociable, and became the most popular man
on the campus. He loved to sing at the parties and sit

up late at night conversing and joking over a Yorkshire pie. There was one redeeming feature of his tenure at Cambridge: it was there he met such lifelong friends as Thomas Gisborne and, more important, William Pitt.

Amid all the merriment of college, Wilberforce's uncle William had died, leaving his estate to him. With the addition of his deceased father's inheritance, William was a wealthy young man with his entire future ahead of him. So what would he do? He had three options: a life of pleasure, a life of business, or a life of politics. He could, if he chose, live the life of a country gentleman, whiling away his hours in hunting, gambling, and socializing. On the other hand, he could return to Hull and become a merchant like his father. Last, like Pitt, he could make a run for Parliament.

His decision, we now know, would alter the course of world history.

# NIGHTINGALE OF THE COMMONS

*T*HE SAME YEAR THAT WILBERFORCE was born, British general James Wolfe captured Quebec, and the English defeated the French in crucial land and sea battles. A few years earlier General Robert Clive had won the Battle of Plassey, thereby establishing Britain's predominance in India. By 1760 French Canada and Spanish Florida were ceded to Britain; and thus, as if by accident, Britain became an empire.[18] Not surprisingly, she was ill prepared for her trusteeship. The fiasco in the American Colonies, engineered by George III and Prime Minister North, led to a war that was then considered a tragedy.

During this time, Wilberforce and Pitt met in the gallery of the House of Commons and listened to the intense debates over America and India. The king and Parliament then governed Britain. The king alone appointed the prime minister, while the Parliament consisted of two houses:

the Lords and the Commons. The Lords, or the upper house, were either hereditary or appointed by the king. They could propose legislation and veto any legislation initiated in the Commons. The Commons, or the lower house, were elected by "freemen" from either counties or boroughs. The Commons, moreover, held the power of the purse, since any tax legislation had to originate there. Both Houses were comprised of members from two political parties. The Whigs were the broadly aristocratic party, and had held office from 1714 until 1770. The Tories were considered the "reform" or "opposition" party, and their ascendancy to power coincided with the careers of Wilberforce and Pitt, both of whom decided, in 1780, to run for Parliament.

Wilberforce returned to Hull in August of 1780 to celebrate his birthday and his coming of age. It just so happened that he was also canvassing the electors of Hull. With a large ox roast and many hogsheads of ale, he wooed (today we might say "bribed") the electors. His opponents were Lord Robert Manners, who stood for the government, and David Hartley, who really represented the landed interests of Lord Rockingham. Wilberforce's charm, fluency, and family name overcame any doubts about his youth and inexperience. When the poll was taken on September 11, he received 1,126 votes, the same number as his two opponents combined. Thus, Wilberforce and Manners were elected to Parliament. Pitt, on the other hand, had been defeated for the seat at Cambridge but was given the "rotten borough" of Appleby by Sir James Lowther.

Pitt and Wilberforce resumed their friendship amid the work of Parliament and the whirl of London society. Pitt immediately took the political lead. Within a few weeks he made his maiden speech on financial reform, a speech much praised by both Burke and North. In June and December, he made stinging attacks on the American War. Only six months later he was made Chancellor of the Exchequer in Shelburne's administration. Wilberforce could hardly keep pace with his brilliant friend. His own maiden speech of May 17, 1781, was devoted to local affairs in Hull. It was not until February 1782 that he launched out into wider waters. He spoke out against the American War, claiming that the government's ministers were acting more like lunatics than statesmen. Speaking in support of General Conway's proposal to end the war, he accused them of conducting the war in a "cruel, bloody and impractical manner."[19] Lord North's administration would never, Wilberforce complained, bring either peace or happiness to Britain.

Meanwhile, Wilberforce and Pitt were making their entrance into fashionable London society. Pitt, being the son of the First Earl of Chatham, was already well connected. Wilberforce, however, did not know "a single person above the rank of commoner."[20] He need not worry. His wealth, charm, and wit swung open society's doors. His mimicry of North was famously funny, and his melodious voice won him the epithet "Nightingale of the House of Commons." What Wilberforce found when he entered London society was a fraternity of wealth, talent, and fame. Great political families such as the Cavendishes, the Howards, the Foxes, and others, dined in palatial houses around town and lived in a state of "jaded hedonism."[21] Along with Pitt and others he hobnobbed with the elite, patronized the theater to see Garrick and Siddons, and attended operas and concerts. More consequentially for his political career, he spent much of his time in the clubs.

The clubs of London were more than casinos and social clubs. They were political societies where members met to discuss plans and legislation. The Tories herded at White's, while the Whigs gathered at Brooks'. Wilberforce, not being a party man, joined both. He also joined Boodle's and several other clubs. Goostrees was his favorite. He and Pitt dined there regularly, and many Cambridge acquaintances—men like Edward Eliot, Henry Bankes, Pepper Arden, and Gerard Edwards—gathered there to drink and play faro. Wilberforce was good at gaming but gave it up for the sake of his victims. He was a highly "clubbable" man.

In the spring and summer it was common for Pitt, Arden, and Eliot to stay with Wilberforce at Lauriston House, the Wimbledon villa he inherited from his uncle. He thought nothing at this time of staying up all night drinking and foining with his friends, just as in his college days.

In September 1783, with the Treaty of Paris concluded, affairs in the Commons gave Wilberforce, Pitt, and Eliot a break to take a continental tour. They headed for France, visiting Rheims, Paris, and Fontainebleau. In Paris, they met the American diplomat Benjamin Franklin and the French patriot Marquis de la Fayette. Marie Antoinette charmed Wilberforce with her "engaging manner and appearance," while Louis XVI struck him as "a clumsy, strange figure in immense boots."[22] Anglo-

French relations were occasionally topics of discussion, but mainly the Englishmen were there for a diversion from Parliament.

Unfortunately, the vacation ended suddenly in late October when the king summoned Pitt to London. The government was on the brink of a crisis.

# THE MIGHTY SHRIMP

*B*ACK IN LONDON, George III was eager to rid himself of the detested North-Fox coalition. He found his chance when Fox proposed his East India Bill. Despite some useful features, the bill created a large board of commissioners who were sworn to be loyal to the coalition. This abysmal pit of patronage incensed the king and he intervened in the Lords to see that the bill was defeated. He then dismissed the coalition. On December 19, 1783, he appointed Pitt, at the age of twenty-four, to be prime minister.

Fox, in the meantime, used the full force of his sarcastic and witty rhetoric to defeat all the new prime minister's motions in Commons. There was wide support for Pitt throughout the country, but without strong support in the Commons, Pitt could not endure in office. Thus, in March Parliament was dissolved for a general election in the hope that a majority of Pittites would be returned.

Wilberforce headed for Yorkshire to canvass for Pitt. Meanwhile, Christopher Wyvill, who had earlier formed the Yorkshire Association for constitutional reform, called a meeting of the freeholders in order to draft an address to the throne for a general election. He set the meeting for March 25 in the grassy yard of York Castle. It was a cold and blustery day, and when Wilberforce arrived he found four thousand freeholders assembled, along with a number of Whig lords such as the duke of Devonshire, Lord John Cavendish, and Lord Surrey, each of whom had been supporters of the North-Fox coalition. The meeting, noted the *York Chronicle,* was "more numerous and respectable than any ever held upon a similar occasion."[23]

The speeches began at midmorning and lasted until late afternoon. Around four o'clock in the afternoon Wilberforce mounted a table to address the weather-beaten audience in support of the address and Pitt. Fighting the wind and rain, he told his listeners that he supported the prerogative of the Crown, denounced the coalition for the odious East India Bill, and warned the freeholders that they were, in fact, facing a constitutional crisis. A messenger, who handed him a letter written in Pitt's own hand, interrupted his speech: Parliament was to be prorogued that very day. He quickly read the letter and announced to the audience that the king had that very moment appealed to the nation's decision.

According to a newspaper account:

> *Mr. Wilberforce made a most argumentative and eloquent speech, which was listened to with the*

*most eager attention, and received with the loudest*
*acclamations of applause. It was indeed a reply to*
*everything that had been said against the Address;*
*but there was such an exquisite choice of expres-*
*sion, and pronounced with such rapidity, that we*
*are unable to do it justice in any account we can*
*give of it. . . .*[24]

Boswell, later famous for his biography of Samuel Johnson, was present and reported: "I saw what seemed a mere shrimp mount the table; but as I listened, he grew, and grew, until the shrimp became a whale."[25] The meeting approved the address amid cries of "We'll have this man for our County Member."[26]

Afterward the Pittites gathered at the York Tavern in St. Helen's Square to discuss their choices for Commons. They were sorely divided between those who supported the association and those who did not; those who were Whigs and those who were Tories; those who were aristocrats and those who were merchants. Their only point of unity, it seems, was their dislike for the North-Fox coalition. They debated and drank late into the night. Quarrels broke out, which Wilberforce helped to quell. Indeed, his eloquence and diplomacy had so impressed the Pittites that at midnight there was a spontaneous cry: "Wilberforce and liberty!" The next day Wilberforce headed for Hull to canvass, and on April 1 was easily reelected. When he returned to York, he found that his supporters had canvassed the county and he was ahead by a healthy margin. His opponents wisely withdrew. On April 6, he was crowned with the "little kingdom" of

Yorkshire, one of the two most powerful seats in Commons.

Wilberforce exulted in his victory. "Keep your Cornish Boroughs" he wrote to Eliot, who had promised him a rotten borough in case he lost Yorkshire. Pitt wrote to applaud him. "My dear Wilberforce, I can never congratulate you on such glorious success."[27] It was, indeed, a magnificent achievement.

From all appearances, Wilberforce was now destined for a dazzling political career. Only twenty-four years old, he had captured one of the most coveted seats in Parliament. Moreover, he was eloquent in debate, secure in wealth, liked by both parties in Parliament, and accepted in London society. Better yet, he was the new prime minister's best friend. Preference and power were in his grasp. Everything flowed in his favor. The stars aligned over his head.

No one—not even Wilberforce himself—could have imagined that he was about to undergo a radical change. A change so revolutionary that he would willingly throw away his promising future. What could be better than the luxury of London society? What better than the power of Parliament? What better than the sinecure of statesmanship?

There was something better, as Wilberforce was soon to discover.

# Religion in the Soul

*T*HE FOX SUPPORTERS LOST more than one hundred seats in the general election. Pitt was now
ascendant in Commons with Wilberforce at his side.
They worked on reform of the parliamentary franchise
in the summer of 1784; but due to Fox's machinations,
they made little progress. They shelved the issue as the
summer session closed.

Meanwhile, Wilberforce had so thoroughly enjoyed
his previous tour to France that he decided to visit the
Continent again. After celebrating his twenty-fifth birthday at the York races, he went to Scarborough where he
ran into Isaac Milner. On a whim, Wilberforce invited
Milner to accompany him, his mother, and his sister to
the Franco-Italian Riviera for the winter. Milner accepted.

Milner, it should be recalled, had taught Wilberforce back at Hull Grammar School. After that he took
his degree from Queen's College, Cambridge, in 1774,
was ordained a year later, and returned to Queen's as a

fellow. Milner was clearly a genius. At the age of eight he had built and designed a sundial, and when still Bachelor of Arts he was elected to the Royal Society. He became a professor of both natural philosophy and mathematics, as well as a distinguished divine. As a wit and conversationalist, he ranked with Samuel Johnson. His conversation, noted Wilberforce, "was lively and dashing."[28] His huge frame matched his immense mind. He was, said one who knew him, "the most enormous man it was ever my fate to see in a drawing room."[29]

In October the party set off for France. With the ladies in one carriage and the "odd couple" in the other, they crossed France to Lyons and sailed down the Rhone to Avignon, where they stayed at St. Omers' Inn. In spite of the deplorable roads they made their way to Marseilles and then headed for Nice. On the way, Milner and Wilberforce occasionally discussed religious topics. By this point in his life, Wilberforce had rejected the Methodist influence of his Wimbledon days; and, thanks to the preaching of Theopilius Lindsey at Essex Chapel, he was essentially a Unitarian or Deist. Milner, on the other hand, was orthodox in his doctrine and evangelical in his persuasion. Wilberforce treated religious subjects flippantly and referred to Methodists as vulgar and unlearned. "If you really want to discuss these subjects seriously," Milner scolded his friend, "I will gladly enter on them with you."[30]

A fashionable resort spot, Nice was frequented by many English visitors. When they arrived there, Wilberforce found such friends as the duke of Gloucester, Lady Rivers, Lady Charlotte, and others. They spent the winter in intellectual idleness—dining, partying, and hiking. One of their party, a Bessy Smith, had a copy of Phillip Doddridge's *The Rise and Progress of Religion in the Soul.*[31] Wilberforce picked it up and asked Milner's opinion. "It is one of the best books ever written. Let us take it with us and read it on our journey."[32] And that they did.

In response to a letter from Pitt urging him to be back in Commons for a motion on reform, they left the ladies at a villa in Nice and headed home. The journey was at times slow and perilous due to snow, but Wilberforce and Milner, huddled in their carriage, spent their time reading and discussing Doddridge. By the time they arrived in London in February 1785, Wilberforce had undergone at least an intellectual conversion. He discarded his Deism and was now giving mental assent to biblical notions of God, Christ, and fallen humanity.

After a short session that focused on reform and Ireland, Wilberforce, with Milner in his carriage, set off to retrieve his family from the Continent. They joined the ladies in Genoa and proceeded through Savoy and Switzerland. Along the way, Wilberforce and Milner studied the Greek New Testament. One by one, Wilberforce's doubts and objections vanished. Conviction was settling upon him. By October he was rising early to pray. He was now clearly going through a real conversion of soul: "As soon as I reflected seriously upon these subjects the deep guilt and black ingratitude of my past life forced itself upon me in the strongest colours, and I condemned myself for having wasted my precious time, and opportunities, and talents."[33]

When he returned to Wimbledon in November, he was in spiritual turmoil and emotional anguish. Now that his eyes were open, he saw with keen vision his own sinfulness. As he later wrote:

> *It was not so much the fear of punishment by which I was affected, as a sense of my great sinfulness in having so long neglected the unspeakable mercies of my God and Saviour; and such was the effect which this thought produced, that for months I was in a state of the deepest depression, from strong convictions of my guilt. Indeed nothing which I have ever read in the accounts of others, exceeded what I then felt.*[34]

His journal at this time records his inner trial. On November 27 he wrote: "I must awake to my dangerous state, and never be at rest till I have made my peace with God. My heart is so hard, my blindness so great, that I cannot get a due hatred of sin, though I see I am all corrupt, and blinded to the perception of spiritual things." The next day: "True, Lord, I am wretched, and miserable, and blind, and naked. What infinite love, that Christ should die to save such a sinner, and how necessary is it He should save us altogether, that we may appear before God with nothing of our own!"[35]

He decided that he needed to talk with two people, one a stranger, the other a dear friend. His friend Pitt came first. On November 24 Pitt called at Wimbledon and the two of them discussed Butler's *Analogy*. This was but a prelude to his letter to Pitt in which he related both his conversion to Christ and his intention to withdraw from worldly society, perhaps even politics itself. He was sure that this revelation would destroy his friendship with Pitt. He was pleasantly surprised, however, when Pitt replied on December 2. First, he reassured Wilberforce of his deep affection:

> *As to any public conduct which your opinion may ever lead you I will not disguise to you that few things could go nearer my heart than to find myself differing from you on any great principle. I trust and believe that it is a circumstance which can hardly occur. But if ever it should, and even if I should experience as much pain in such an event as I have hitherto encouragement and pleasure in the reverse, believe me it is impossible that it should shake the sentiments of affection and friendship which I bear towards you, and which I must be forgetful and insensible indeed if I ever could part with. They are sentiments engraved on my heart, and will never be effaced or weakened.*[36]

Pitt then challenged the idea that Wilberforce should withdraw from public life. "You will not suspect me of thinking lightly of any moral or religious motives which guide you," he wrote. "But forgive me if I cannot help expressing my fear that you are deluding yourself into principles which have but too much tendency to counteract your own object, and to render your virtues and your talents useless both to yourself and to mankind." The "delusion," according to Pitt, was the notion that

Christianity required strict seclusion and private meditation only. "Surely the principles as well as the practice of Christianity are simple, and lead not to meditation only, but to action."[37] Pitt, of course, was right, as Wilberforce would soon see. The next day the two met and Pitt tried to argue Wilberforce out of his convictions, but to no avail. Nonetheless, he did persuade Wilberforce to see that "as far as I could conform to the world, with a perfect regard to my duty to God, myself and my fellows, I was bound to do it."[38]

The second person Wilberforce had to talk with was John Newton. At Milner's urging, he wrote to Newton requesting an interview. Newton was by then sixty years old, and a well-known evangelical preacher within the Established Church. As a young man he had been impressed into the navy and eventually became a slave trader. While in this degraded occupation he met Christ. Some years later he left the trade, entered holy orders, and became a friend of the famous poet Cowper. It was through Newton's ministry that Wilberforce began to find serenity. "Very unhappy," he notes in his diary, "called at Newton's, and bitterly moved: *comforted me*."[39] After meeting with Newton on December 7, Wilberforce records, "When I came away, I found my mind in a calm and tranquil state."[40]

Like Pitt, Newton advised Wilberforce not to withdraw from public life. "It is hoped and believed that the Lord has raised you up for the good of His church and for the good of the nation."[41]

A more prophetic word could not have been spoken.

# Two Great Objects

*I*N 1786, WILBERFORCE RETURNED TO PARLIAMENT a changed man. He found the peace and serenity of true Christianity while looking for his new life's calling. The first evidence of change was his resignation from the clubs. He gave up gambling and dancing, as well as going to the theater. Perforce he still had to mix with fashionable society, although now he was less comfortable and more conscientious of his conversation, eating, and idleness. He feared that his altered behavior might "excite disgust rather than cordiality," but his affable character and charm made him a welcome guest.[42] It was simply not in his nature to be a prig.

He also began a journal to aid his spiritual growth, which reflects his attempt to be moderate while mixing with London's elite. For instance, an entry for December 1786 states his "resolutions" to be "temperate." These resolutions were "made in the sight of God, and will, I would humbly hope, be adhered to." He then promised to "every night note down" whether he had kept them or not, and "at the end of every week set down on this paper whether in the course of it I have in any instance clearly transgressed."[43]

His changed life was evident to others, especially his family. His mother, who had earlier been so alarmed by his childhood "Methodism," was now concerned that he would become a recluse. He reassured her by letter: "This would merit no better name than desertion, and if I were thus to fly from the part where Providence has placed me, I know not how I could look for the blessing of God upon my retirement; and without this heavenly assistance, either in the world or in solitude, our own endeavours will be equally ineffectual." But she was not fully persuaded until he visited in October. His pleasantness and cheerfulness were winsome. "If this be madness," said her friend Mrs. Sykes, "I hope he will bite us all."[44]

Wilberforce's conversion led him to view society in an entirely different manner. After being defeated, in 1786, in his attempt to soften some of the savage features of the penal code, he began to realize that the best deterrent to crime was a general reformation of moral conduct. As he wrote to his friend Wyvill: "The most effectual way of preventing the greater crimes is by punishing the smaller, and by endeavouring to suppress the general spirit of licentiousness which is the parent of every species of vice."[45]

The "parent" was quite fecund indeed. Drunkenness, among both the upper and lower classes, was a national epidemic. While the poor drowned their sorrows with gin, the rich sailed on a sea of claret. Fox and

Sheridan were commonly drunk in Commons, and not even Pitt escaped this vice. Corruption and immorality were prevalent in the highest ranks, including the royal family. Gambling, as we have seen, was widespread and accepted. Dueling was condoned. Prostitution was pandemic. In London at this time, one of every four unmarried women was a prostitute. Worse still, there were special brothels for females under fourteen to satisfy the depraved lusts of wealthy lechers. Prison records show that the average age of a prostitute in London was sixteen.[46]

Upon reading the *History of the Society for the Reformation of Manners in the Year 1692*, by Joseph Woodward, Wilberforce got the idea to found a similar organization to deal with the moral decay engulfing England. He enlisted notables from the influential classes such as the duke of Montagu, the archbishop of Canterbury, and Lord North; even Pitt himself approved the plan. In addition to Wilberforce, Edward Eliot, and Sir Middleton, the first committee meeting consisted of six dukes, eleven lesser peers, nineteen archbishop, and bishops, and a dozen commoners. The king endorsed the idea and thus made a royal proclamation against vice and immorality in June 1787.

Copies of the proclamation were then distributed to magistrates throughout the country as Wilberforce began to write letters and personally visit civil and ecclesiastical leaders urging them to set up local chapters of the Proclamation Society. Though some leaders, such as Lord Fitzwilliam, laughed in Wilberforce's face, others took the proclamation seriously and began to enforce long- neglected laws against drunkenness, obscenity, and other vices. Thus began one of Wilberforce's two great objects.

The other, of course, was the slave trade. While at Hull, Wilberforce received a letter from Sir Charles Middleton, comptroller of the navy and a member of Parliament, urging him to consider the issue of the slave trade. Middleton was also an Evangelical and an ardent abolitionist. His wife, by the way, was an accomplished artist and friend to Hannah More, the playwright. James Ramsay, who had served under Middleton as a surgeon in the navy, had influenced his views on the trade. Ramsay had attended a slave ship where an epidemic was raging, and was horrified at what he saw. He told Middleton about the suffering he witnessed, and later wrote a book, *Essay on the Treatment and Conversion of African Slaves in the British Sugar Colonies*, exposing the brutality of the trade. Ramsay also recruited Thomas Clarkson to the abolitionist cause. Clarkson, like Wilberforce, had attended St. John's, and while there wrote a prize essay on slavery, "The Slavery and Commerce of the Human Species," which was later published. Granville Sharp, who, as we will see shortly, was famous for his adjudication of the *Somerset* case, was another of the abolitionists who gathered around Middleton at his home at Teston.

And it was to Teston that Wilberforce was invited early in 1787. We have no record of the conversation, but we know that the small group of abolitionists urged Wilberforce to become their parliamentary leader. He was inclined but thought perhaps a better-qualified person could be found. A little later Clarkson personally lobbied him. Quite naturally, Wilberforce discussed the matter with Pitt, who urged him: "Do not lose time, or the ground may be occupied by another."[47] Soon afterward, Clarkson arranged a dinner at the home of his friend Bennet Langton, who was a friend of Samuel Johnson. Sir Joshua Reynolds, Boswell, Middleton, and Windham were present, and all encouraged Wilberforce to take leadership in Commons on the subject of abolition.

Wilberforce had heard the opinion of men; now he waited to hear the voice of God. In the meantime, Sharp, Clarkson, and others officially established the Committee for the Abolition of the Slave Trade in May 1787; and throughout the summer Clarkson investigated the trade. In the autumn, Wilberforce visited Hannah More in Cowslip Green.

Back at home in October, Wilberforce sat in his library on a dark rainy day pondering the evils of the trade. He reviewed Clarkson's tracts. He prayed and meditated. Then the commission came: he heard with certainty the call of God. On the twenty-eighth he dipped his quill pen into its inkwell and jotted in his diary those now immortal words: "God Almighty has set before me two great objects: the suppression of the slave trade and the reformation of manners." The slaves had found their champion.

# THE SLAVES' CHAMPION

*T*HE ABOLITIONISTS WERE FACED with two related evils: the slave trade and the institution of slavery itself. They initially had to decide which to attack first; for all agreed that ideally both should be abolished. After some debate, they decided that the first attack should be on the trade (the goal being *abolition*), and that a successful campaign would lay the groundwork for an attack on slavery itself (the goal being *emancipation*). A premature attack on the institution of slavery might jeopardize any chance of success. Thus, they summarized their aim as follows: "Our immediate aim is, by diffusing a knowledge of the subject, and particularly the Modes of pro-curing and treating slaves, to interest men of every description in the Abolition of the Traffic; but especially those from whom any alteration must proceed—the Members of our Legislature."[48]

The first step for Wilberforce was to educate himself on the trade; in this, Granville Sharp and Thomas Clarkson greatly assisted him. Sharp was already a seasoned abolitionist. As early as 1729 West Indian planters had appealed to the Crown for the return of slaves who had run away on English soil while they, the planters, were visiting various English ports. They received the verdict they desired: neither residence in England nor baptism affected a master's right and property. A runaway slave must be returned to his master and could be compelled to return to the West Indian plantations.

Sharp, however, was to put this law to the test. In 1765 he had helped a deserted slave, Jonathan Strong, to regain his health, only to have the owner return to claim him and charge Sharp with robbery. This led him to study the law on slavery. For two years he pored over the writings of British legal experts and consulted many lawyers, including the famous jurist Blackstone. In the published results of his research, *The Injustice and Dangerous Tendency of Tolerating Slavery in England,* Sharp argued that under British common law slavery was impermissible, and thus every slave entering England should be free. While his tract was making waves in legal circles, in 1772 Sharp brought forward the case of James Somerset, another runaway slave. The case was heard in three sittings and aroused great public interest. English history was in the making. Though the presiding judge, Chief Justice Mansfield, one of the greatest jurists of his day, had tried to cajole the disputants to drop the case, a judgment was inevitable. On June 22, 1772, he delivered a stunning verdict: "Tracing the subject to natural

principles, the claim of slavery never can be supported.
The power claimed [slavery] never was in use here or
acknowledged by the law. . . . The State of Slavery . . . is
so odious that nothing can be suffered to support it but
positive law. Whatever inconveniences therefore may
follow from the decision, I cannot say this case is allowed
or approved by the law of England: and therefore the
black must be discharged."[49] In effect, and in law, slavery
was now illegal in the British Isles.

The British colonies, however, were another matter.
The ruling did not affect them. And here, Clarkson's role
became so important. Throughout the summer of 1787
Clarkson traveled to London, Bristol, Liverpool, and elsewhere collecting evidence on the trade: he studied the
size of slave ships, recorded the condition of the Middle
Passage, took testimony from sailors, and bought various
instruments such as shackles and thumbscrews. What
he learned was alarming, to say the least. Slavers often
raided the African coast in search of victims; or, more
often, they bribed local chiefs with trinkets, guns, and
liquor to war on their neighbors and provide the spoils
as barter. Some chiefs began to oppress their own people
by passing laws that carried slavery as the punishment
for minor offenses. Kidnapping became pandemic. Slaves
captured far inland were chained and marched for miles
to the coast. Those who grew ill or weak were left to die;
the slave tracks became strewn with human bones. Once
on the coast, they were beaten and forced to enter the
slave ships. On board they were handcuffed, chained,
and stuffed in shelves with no room to move. During the
Middle Passage from Africa to the West Indies, the slaves

lay for weeks in their own refuse and vomit. The stench of the slave ships cast a foul cloud a mile over the ocean. The sailors often raped the black women, thus the ships were described as "half brothel and half bedlam." Those who died from seasickness or disease were thrown overboard to the trailing sharks.

Those slaves "fortunate" enough to survive the Middle Passage were, upon arrival at their destination, hosed, oiled, and fattened to fetch a good price. Wounds were doctored up and concealed. Stripped naked and chained, they were marched to the auction block. The sick and infirm were lumped with the women and children, and then cheaply sold as "refuse." The unsold slaves were dumped on the shore and left to die. The purchased ones spent the next year going through the process of "seasoning," being disciplined both physically and psychologically for a life of bondage.[50]

The brutality and inhumanity of the trade, which shocked Wilberforce, fortified him with a false optimism. How could such flagrant abuses of humanity be justified? Nevertheless, justified they were. In the meantime, before he could make his maiden abolition speech, he fell deathly ill. He had frequently suffered digestive problems, but the attack in late January 1788 put his life in danger. The assault of piles and constipation was compounded with high fever and an inability to eat. As his condition worsened, Dr. Warren gave notice that the "little fellow with his callico guts, cannot possibly survive a twelve month."[51] Wilberforce's doctors prescribed opium, a drug commonly dispensed in the eighteenth century. After much protest, and out of a deepening sense of desperation, he submitted to the dangerous remedy. Miraculously, it worked, although he was thereafter dependent on it to maintain his health.

In February, the king directed the Committee of the Privy Council to investigate the trade. And while Wilberforce was recuperating at Bath in April, he asked Pitt to move for abolition in Commons. Pitt complied both from personal friendship and from personal conviction. In May he moved for abolition, and the debates took place that summer. William Dolben, a proposed friend of abolition, advanced the Middle Passage Bill, which was to limit the number of slaves that could be carried on a vessel. Its provisions were experimental and temporary, having to be renewed the next year by Parliament. Dolben's Bill, as it was called, passed Commons with ease but was bitterly opposed in the Lords. Only Pitt's threat to resign, should the Lords defeat the Bill, secured its passage by a mere two votes.

If such a modest regulation of the trade brought such vehement resistance, what did this presage for the future of abolition? This was, as Wilberforce soon learned, an omen of the long and bitter struggle to come. For the next eighteen years Wilberforce and his fellow colleagues were to encounter filibustering, technical maneuvers, false testimony, threats, fallacious arguments, and a host of other obstacles to their crusade for abolition.

# OPENING SALVOS

*W*HEN WILBERFORCE ROSE IN PARLIAMENT in May 1789 to give his first abolition speech, the pro-slavery forces had already organized. The battle lines were drawn.

In a speech that lasted three and a half hours, he began by urging the members to be calm and impartial in their reasoning. He was careful not to arouse hostility by accusing any particular member or group: "I mean not to accuse anyone, but to take the shame upon myself, in common indeed with the whole Parliament of Britain, for having suffered this horrid trade to be carried on under their authority. We are all guilty. . . ." He then reminded his hearers that the evidence was before the Privy Council and the facts were before the House. No other evidence was needed. The horrors of the Middle Passage were laid before their eyes and indisputable. The slave ships were a graveyard for British seamen. "More sailors die in one year in the Slave Trade," he said, "than die in two years in all the other trades put together." By abolishing the trade, the planters would be led to treat their slaves more humanely, which in turn would produce, over time, a stronger work force. To the objection that the French would take over if Britain abandoned the trade, Wilberforce suggested that Britain ought to take the lead and set the example for the rest of Europe. Total abolition was the only noble course of action:

> I trust . . . I have proved that, upon every ground, total abolition ought to take place. I have urged many things which are not my own leading motives for proposing it, since I have wished to show every description of gentlemen, and particularly the West India planters, who deserve every attention, that the abolition is politic upon their own principles. Policy, however, Sir, is not my principle, and I am not ashamed to say it. There is a principle above everything that is politic, and when I reflect on the command which says: "Thou shalt do no murder," believing its authority to be divine, how can I dare to set up any reasonings of my own against it?

He then urged Parliament to act with justice in light of the truth:

> Sir, the nature and all the circumstance of this Trade are now laid open to us. We can no longer plead ignorance. We cannot evade it. We may spurn it. We may kick it out of the way. But we cannot turn aside so as to avoid seeing it. For it is brought

> *now so directly before our eyes that this House*
> *must decide and must justify to all the world and*
> *to its own conscience, the rectitude of the ground*
> *of its decision. . . . Let not Parliament be the only*
> *body that is insensible to the principles of natural*
> *justice.*[52]

Though such giants as Burke, Pitt, and Fox supported him, Commons was not swayed. When the debate
resumed nine days later, the House passed a motion to
reject the evidence of the Privy Council and to constitute
its own committee to hear evidence in the summer. This
was simply a delay tactic. Throughout the remainder of
this year and the next, Wilberforce sat on the committee hearing testimony and evidence. In the autumn of
1790, he cloistered at Gisborne's Yoxall Lodge studying
the trade. For nearly two months, he and Thomas Babington spent nine or more hours a day poring over the 1,400
pages of evidence that had already been presented to the
House. They slept little and ate even less.

In 1791 the committee reconvened in February, and
it was that same month that the Methodist John Wesley
sent a letter of encouragement to Wilberforce:

> *My dear sir,*
> *Unless the Divine Power has raised you up to be an*
> Athanasius contra mundum *I see not how you can*
> *go through with your glorious enterprise in oppos-*
> *ing that execrable villainy which is the scandal of*
> *religion, of England and of human nature. Unless*
> *God has raised you up for this very thing, you will*

> *be worn out by the opposition of men and devils;*
> *but if God is with you, who can be against you? Are*
> *all of them stronger than God? Oh, be not weary*
> *in well-doing. Go on, in the name of God and in*
> *the power of His might, till even American slavery,*
> *the vilest that ever saw the sun, shall vanish away*
> *before it. . . . That he who has guided you from your*
> *youth up, may continue to strengthen you in this*
> *and in all things, is the prayer of*
> *Dear Sir, your affectionate servant,*
> *John Wesley* [53]

In April, in a speech that lasted four hours, Wilberforce again thundered in the House for abolition:

> *Never, never will we desist till we have wiped away*
> *this scandal from the Christian name, released our-*
> *selves from the load of guilt under which we at*
> *present labour, and extinguish every trace of this*
> *bloody traffic, of which our posterity, looking back*
> *to the history of these enlightened times, will scarce*
> *believe that it has been suffered to exist so long a*
> *disgrace and dishonour to this country.* [54]

The slave interests were not about to back down, however. One proslavery member argued that abolition would bring economic disaster:

> *Abolition would instantly annihilate a trade, which*
> *annually employed upwards of 5,500 sailors,*
> *upwards of 160 ships, and whose exports amount*

*to 800,000 sterling; and would undoubtedly bring the West India trade to decay, whose exports and imports amount to upwards of 6,000,000 sterling, and which give employment in upwards of 160,000 tons of additional shipping, and sailors in proportion.*[55]

After a dramatic pause, he then looked to the West Indian owners in the gallery and, pointing at them, shouted: "These are my masters." Another defender of the trade unwittingly showed the heartlessness of his position when he admitted that it "was not an amiable trade, but neither was the trade of a butcher . . . and yet a mutton chop was, nevertheless, a very good thing."[56]

For two days a fierce battle ensued, with members arguing and shouting at one another. Again supported by Fox, Burke, and other leaders, the debate was described as a battle between the giants and the pygmies. The giants won the argument, but the pygmies outnumbered them. As one cynical observer commented, "Commerce clinked its purse."[57] The motion lost.

# BLACK TERROR, RED TERROR

*I*T WAS NOW APPARENT THAT THE STRUGGLE would be long and bitter, so Henry Thornton suggested to Wilberforce that he, Sharp, Macaulay, Clarkson, Gisborne, and others gather at his home in Clapham to consider their strategy. Clapham was four miles south of Westminster, and Thornton's home was a picturesque Queen Anne manor called Battersea Rise, overlooking the grassy Clapham Common. The large oval-shaped library, designed by Pitt, became the headquarters where they held many cabinet meetings and spent hours together in prayer. Clapham was to be Wilberforce's home for many years to follow.

Having been spurned by the House, the Saints turned to the masses. In the summer the Committee for Abolition began to mobilize public opinion. The war of pamphlets was on. They produced a one-volume abridgment of the House, evidence to be distributed to their network of local chapters. Clarkson reproduced a drawing of the Brookes, showing the horrendous conditions of the Middle Passage. The Christian poet Cowper wrote his *Negro's Complaint,* which was distributed with the special inscription, "A Subject for Conversation at the Tea-table."

> *Is there, as ye sometimes tell us,*
> *Is there One who reigns on high?*
> *Has He bid you buy and sell us*
> *Speaking from His throne, the sky?*
> *Ask Him if your knotted scourges,*
> *Matches, blood-extorting screws,*
> *Are the means that duty urges*
> *Agents of His will to use?*

Josiah Wedgwood produced a cameo of a chained Negro begging for compassion: "Am I not a Man and a Brother?" These were distributed widely, set in bracelets and pins, and worn by ladies of fashion. For once, commented Clarkson, fashion was "in the honourable office of promoting the cause of justice, humanity and freedom."[58] Because of the public campaign, petitions against the trade began to flood Commons: 310 from England, 187 from Scotland, and 20 from Wales. All demanded abolition. Only five favored the slave trade.

Backed by public opinion, Wilberforce addressed the House in late 1792, painting for them the bleak reality of the Middle Passage:

> *In the year 1788 in a ship in this trade, 650 persons*
> *were on board, out of whom 155 died. In another,*

> *405 were on board, out of whom were lost 200. In another there were on board 402, out of whom 73 died. When Captain Wilson was asked the causes of this mortality, he replied that the slaves had a fixed melancholy and defection; that they wished to die; that they refused all sustenance, till they were beaten in order to compel them to eat; and that when they had been so beaten, they looked in the faces of the whites, and said, piteously, "Soon we shall be no more."* [59]

Wilberforce's motion for abolition was modified by the word *gradual*. Nevertheless, the motion passed. With the public behind him, victory seemed attainable.

Yet just as the abolitionists seemed to be mounting an invincible offensive, events turned against them. In August of 1791 the slaves in St. Dominique rose in rebellion, massacred their masters, and gained control of much of the country. A three-way war between whites, mulattos, and blacks raged with terrifying cruelty. When word reached England in early 1792, the anti-abolitionists used the news to spread fear and confusion. The slave revolts in Martinique and Domicia were likewise blamed on the abolitionists. Now the planters had a strong emotional argument for not tampering with the trade. The "Black Terror" proved a great obstacle to abolition for many years thereafter.

Worse still was the "Red Terror." The storming of the Bastille in Paris in 1789 was initially greeted with optimism by some of the abolitionists. They hoped the claims of liberty and equality would be extended to blacks. Yet, the September massacres turned the Revolution into a Reign of Terror. The guillotine's appetite was insatiable as the streets of France flowed with blood. With the execution of Louis XVI in January 1793, the British Parliament hardened to any talk of abolition. Pitt's administration, originally friendly toward reform and abolition, now became progressively repressive. Samuel Romilly described the deadly impact of the Revolution on Parliament: "If any person be desirous of having an adequate idea of the mischievous effects which have been produced in this country by the French Revolution and all its attendant horrors, he should attempt some reform on humane and liberal principles. . . . He will then find not only what a stupid spirit of conservation, but what a savage spirit, it has infused into the minds of his countrymen."[60]

Civil unrest in England in the autumn of 1792 was thought linked to the Revolution. In February 1793, France declared war on Britain, and notions of liberty, democracy, and republicanism were branded as atheistic and revolutionary. And that included abolition. As the earl of Abingdon fumed, "What does the abolition of the slave trade mean? more or less in effect, than liberty and equality? what more or less than the rights of man? and what is liberty and equality; and what the rights of man, but the foolish fundamental principles of this new philosophy?"[61] The hardships of the war, as well as a series of hard winters and bad harvests in 1795–96, led to further unrest and the revitalization of radical clubs. Jacobin agitation spread. The radical London Corresponding Society, which had already distributed nearly 200,000 copies of Paine's *Rights of Man,* garnered a crowd of

150,000 people and called for civil war. Two days later mobs assaulted the king's carriage. Pitt feared the guillotine. Even Wilberforce himself began to feel that the very foundations of society were cracking: "I greatly fear some civil war or embroilment."[62]

Parliament responded with force. In November, bills against treasonable practices and seditious meetings were debated and passed. Any political meeting could number no more than fifty people, and any seditious speech was grounds for immediate arrest. Wilberforce supported these bills as a "temporary sacrifice" until the storm passed. He traveled to Castle Yard in York to convince his constituents of the need for these measures. By 1796 the membership in the radical clubs was waning.

Unfortunately, so was enthusiasm for abolition. Revolt and revolution doomed reform.

# Manners and Marriage

*W*ILBERFORCE BELIEVED THAT HIS ATTEMPTS at political and social reform would never succeed
unless there was a moral renovation of society. London
was one vast casino where drunken "gentlemen" lost
their fortunes at the table, while others lost their lives in
duels. The wealthy were nearly insensible to moral sua-
sion. The poor, on the other hand, were ground to dust
by the encroaching machinery of the industrial revolution. Sickly children labored in noxious conditions only
to have their parents waste their meager income on gin.
Hospitals teemed with vermin while prisons overflowed
with criminals.

As early as 1789, shortly after his divine call to
"reform the manners" of the nation, Wilberforce contem-
plated writing a book on practical Christianity. His object
was to influence the religious conduct and "manners"
(that is, morals) of the upper classes. In a memorandum

dated December 6, 1789, he made a list of pros and cons for publishing his manifesto. In its favor, he speculated that it might open a way to speak to "the careless whom I know," to whom "I can hardly open myself with plainness, in private." Also, "the really well-disposed could be taught the difference between being almost and altogether Christians." In writing, "things may be said to those in high stations, bishops, &c., which could hardly be personally [said] to them in private." Moreover, "My way [would be] cleared of many difficulties by this explicit avowal of my sentiments; unjust conclusions will no longer be drawn from my cheerfulness, or my not making religion the matter of frequent conversation." And last, "perhaps an association of serious people [would be] produced, labouring for national reform."[63]

On the contrary, Wilberforce reasoned that he could accomplish many of these objectives "without publication, by private conversation with friends, and by public declarations." He also feared being considered "over-righteous" or "an enthusiast," which would "deter people from co-operating with me for national reform." There was also the possibility he might lose his "influence with Pitt . . . and other great men, even King George himself. . . . I should be looked upon as morose and uncharitable. Bishops would fear me." As he surveyed the state of the nation, he concluded that an association for reform "would not now do good; the times would not bear it—the courts of law would set their faces against it."[64]

After much deliberation, Wilberforce decided against writing and publishing his sentiments, at least for now. However, he did leave it as an option for the future: "I resolve on the whole not to publish, but I may at leisure write, and leave an injunction to publish if I die. Then much of the good may be done by the work, at least some of it, and none of the evil accrue."[65]

"Leisure" was hardly a commodity that Wilberforce had in store. With the activities of the Proclamation Society and the Abolition Committee, as well as his ongoing duties as a member of Parliament during a time of war and unrest, he was nearly stretched beyond his limits. Nevertheless, in 1793 he began to write. "I laid the first timbers of my tract," he noted in his diary. During the summer recess of 1794 he began "thinking in earnest about my tract. Here for the first time I have got a little quiet, and have resumed my work diligently; yet I doubt whether I can do anything worth publishing." Confronted with writer's block he moaned, "I stare at my subject instead of closing with it."[66]

The summer of 1796 was a busy time. He was reelected for York in June. He labored with Pitt and Dundas on a possible treaty with France. He lobbied for the construction of more churches; he raised funds for the war-poor; and he worked on prison and hospital reform. In December he helped to establish the Society for Bettering the Condition of the Poor. Yet, somehow he continued to write. Though he fell ill in January 1797 and had to retire to Bath, when he returned to London in February his tract was sent to the printer. In April, *A Practical View* hit the streets.

Contrary to all expectations the book was a smashing success—a bestseller! Congratulations came pouring in. Lord Muncaster wrote: "As a friend I thank you for it; as a man I doubly thank you; but as a member of the Christian world, I render you all gratitude and acknowledgement." Old John Newton confided to a friend: "What a phenomenon has Mr. Wilberforce sent abroad. *Such* a book, by *such* a man, and at *such* a time!" The "time" to which Newton refers was, of course, a time of great national strife and insecurity in which many looked to religion, and hence Wilberforce, for answers. A former skeptic and devotee of Voltaire wrote to Wilberforce and told him that he had been converted by reading *A Practical View*. That was not an isolated testimony. According to his sons, "Not a year passed throughout his after-life, in which he did not receive fresh testimonies to the blessed effects which it pleased God to produce through his publication."[67]

The book was clearly aimed at the upper and middle classes of society who were either skeptics or mere nominal Christians. Yet only two years later the *Annual Register* reported, "It was a wonder for the lower orders throughout all parts of England, to see the avenues to the churches filled with carriages." Perhaps the most meaningful and touching testimony to the impact of his book came from a Mrs. Crewe. As Edmund Burke lay dying, she later related, he "spent much of the last two days of his life reading Wilberforce's book, and said that he derived much comfort from it, and that if he lived he should thank Wilberforce for having sent such a book into the world."[68]

Wilberforce's star was rising: he was financially independent, politically well connected, and socially influential. He was, as we might say today, a most eligible bachelor. Notwithstanding, only a few months earlier he had expressed his growing sense of loneliness. At age thirty-seven, he conjectured that his marital status would probably never change. "But I must not think of such matters now," he wrote, "it makes me feel my solitary state too sensibly."[69]

As it turned out, the day after his book was released Babington "strongly recommended Miss Spooner for wife for me. We talked about it." Two days later he dined with her and noted in his journal, "*Pleased with Miss Spooner.*" The next week was a whirlwind courtship. He saw Barbara nearly every day while thinking of her constantly. On the sixteenth he writes, "What a blessed Sunday have I been permitted to spend, how happy at dinner and in love." On the twenty-first he confesses, "For first time slept well tonight. Every other [night] kept awake thinking of Miss Spooner." Saturday the twenty-second: "Supped with the Spooners—captivated with Miss Spooner. My heart gone . . ." Indeed, his heart was gone, for the next day he proposed marriage. Thus, only ten days after Babington's prompting, Wilberforce was engaged. On the twenty-third he reflected on the tempestuous week:

> *This last week seems a month. I have constantly . . .*
> *prayed to God for his direction and read his word—*
> *yesterday had resolved to wait before I determined*
> *about Miss Spooner, but she quite captivated me*
> *last night. . . . I could not sleep for thinking of her,*
> *and being much agitated this morning at and after*
> *church, wrote a long rambling letter to her which*

> *she has just returned with favourable answer.* Jacta
> est alea. *I believe she is admirably suited to me,*
> *and there are many circumstances which seem to*
> *advise the step. I trust God will bless me; I go to*
> *pray to Him.*[70]

Friends such as Isaac Milner and Hannah More
advised caution. Others thought Miss Spooner unsuit-
able: it was not a good marriage by "society" standards.
Nevertheless, his mind, or should we say his heart, was
made up. On May 30, 1797, William and Barbara were
married. Over the span of thirty-five years, she brought
him six children and much joy. One of his chief blessings, he later wrote, was "a domestic happiness beyond
what could have been conceived possible."[71] He never
regretted his hasty decision.

# The Arduous Struggle

*A* DARK CLOUD HUNG OVER ENGLAND as the specter of Napoleon haunted the Continent. Victory off Cape St. Vincent on Valentine's Day, 1797, could not compensate for the threat of financial disaster at home when the Bank of England threatened to suspend cash payments. Though the crisis passed, more were to come. In April the navy mutinied at Spithead, and in June at Nore. A French invasion appeared imminent. Napoleon's lightning campaign in Italy drove the British Fleet from the Mediterranean. The French Republic rebuffed offers of peace. Jubilation over Nelson's victory at the Nile in 1798 was short-lived. In their voracious march through the Continent, the French broke the Austrians while also conquering southern Germany.

The same year, Pitt almost lost his life in a foolish duel with George Tierney, a radical member of Parliament who insulted him in a debate over the war. Wilberforce was horrified and drafted a motion against dueling to be presented in Commons. Pitt's appeals were heard and, out of concern for the country's stability, Wilberforce refrained from any action that might be construed as an attack on the prime minister.

The general fear of Jacobinism led to severity on the part of Wilberforce and Parliament. In June of 1797, for example, the Proclamation Society prosecuted Thomas Williams for publishing and distributing Paine's *Age of Reason*, a book that spread atheistic and revolutionary principles.[72] Moreover, late in 1798, Parliament debated and passed a bill to continue the Habeas Corpus Suspension Act, which empowered authorities to imprison without trial those suspected dangerous to the State. During the debate, the radical Courtenay complained about prison conditions at Cold Bath Fields. Wilberforce defended the Suspension Act and the prison, but in the latter case, he was wrong. It was later discovered that conditions there were deplorable. The warden, it so happened, intentionally deceived Wilberforce when he had earlier visited the prison. In fact, Wilberforce had a keen concern about prison and penal reform, and reformers such as Elizabeth Fry, John Howard, and Jeremy Bentham considered him a friend. Another stern measure of this period was the Combination Act, passed in June of 1799. "Combinations" of workers—what we today call unions—were considered hotbeds of revolutionary sentiment at a time of national crisis; they were thus outlawed.

In 1801 the question of Catholic emancipation and the income tax forced Pitt's resignation. Addington succeeded him during the brief Peace of Amiens. Bonaparte was triumphant in war and, being a tyrant at heart, strove to dominate Europe. War with Britain was renewed in 1804, and Pitt was restored to office. The following year Pitt's greatest political ally, Lord Melville (Dundas), stood trial for impeachment, having been accused of misappropriating government funds. He was censured and forever lost office. Wilberforce's speech was decisive, and Pitt reeled from losing Dundas, as well as from feeling betrayed by Wilberforce. Less than a year later Pitt was dead.

Throughout this period of turmoil and war, Wilberforce continued his humanitarian projects. In 1799 he helped in the formation of the Church Missionary Society, and in 1800 he proposed legislation to prevent cruelty to animals. He supported a compulsory smallpox vaccination and founded the Society for the Better Observance of the Sabbath. In 1803 he formed a society for the distribution of Bibles, which led to the founding of the British and Foreign Bible Society in March 1804.

His greatest humanitarian project was, of course, abolition. For this he labored incessantly, even though the decade from 1794 to 1804 was a time of famine for the abolitionists. These were the dark years—years of continual and accumulated defeat. The Abolition Committee had only two meetings in the years 1795 through 1797; and from 1798 to 1804, not one meeting was held.

Nevertheless, Wilberforce had promised that he would never desist in the fight until he achieved victory. His motion in 1796 carried through two readings. "Surprise and joy in carrying my question," he wrote.[73] Yet the third reading was defeated when many of his supporters decided to attend a comic opera in London and thus missed the debate. The next year brought another defeat, as well as the death of Wilberforce's friends Edward Eliot and his brother-in-law Dr. Clarke. In 1798, his motion in April was again defeated, and two months later, he learned of his mother's death. The following year Wilberforce's annual motion lost, although a bill to limit trading on certain parts of the African coasts passed. The Lords, however, threw it out.

The new century brought further defeats. In fact, 1800 was the first year since the opening salvos that Wilberforce did not make his annual motion. The West Indian planters had made a false promise to suspend the trade, only to change their minds after it was too late for a motion in Commons. Again, in 1801 no motion was made due to the widespread distress caused by war and bad harvests. Moreover, in 1802 Wilberforce hoped that peace with France would provide an opportunity to urge abolition at a general convention of European powers—a "grand Abolition plan." His dream came to nothing. Reports of insurrections in the West Indies further deterred any motion. He did gain a small victory, however, by defeating Canning's motion to allow the importation of slaves into newly acquired lands such as Trinidad. The next year Wilberforce had determined to make a motion for abolition. But he then fell seriously ill; while recuperating, war with France was renewed, invasion was imminent, and his annual motion was again postponed. "You can conceive what would be said," he wrote to Babington, "if I were to propose the Abolition now."[74]

In 1804, the tide began to change. The Abolition Committee formally reassembled with several new members, such as Lord Brougham, Lord Teignmouth, James Stephen, Thomas Babington Macaulay (the son of Zachary), and Robert Grant (the son of Charles). Thomas Gisborne was a corresponding member. Pitt was back in office and with the passage of the Act of Union, one hundred new Irish members, with no ties to the slave industry, were added to Parliament. In May, Wilberforce's motion for abolition won by an overwhelming majority, 124–49. The bill passed its second and third readings, albeit by smaller majorities, but again the Lords were opposed and the bill was postponed to the following year. Meanwhile, Wilberforce urged Pitt to issue a proclamation prohibiting the importation of slaves into the newly acquired Dutch colonies. Pitt agreed but procrastinated. At the same time, Brougham headed for Europe to put pressure on the Dutch government, Clarkson began to gather more evidence, and Wilberforce worked on an abolition tract.

The session of 1805 dealt the abolitionists a disheartening blow. When Wilberforce made his motion for abolition in February, Pitt avoided the debate and the Irish members either were absent or turned against abolition. The measure was defeated 70 to 77. Wilberforce was crushed. "I never felt so much on any Parliamentary occasion," he wrote. "I could not sleep after first waking at night. The poor blacks rushed into my mind, and the guilt of our wicked land."[75] He continued to press Pitt for a proclamation concerning Guiana, but he delayed.

A few months later, in January 1806, Pitt died, and the Ministry of All the Talents succeeded him: Lord Henry Petty became Chancellor of the Exchequer, and Fox and Grenville came into power, with the new cabinet on the side of abolition. Lord Castlereagh, now Secretary of State, made the long-awaited proclamation Pitt had promised. Moreover, Fox secured resolutions in both Houses condemning the trade, and secured a promise from the Prince Regent not to interfere in the Lords. In May, a bill prohibiting British subjects from engaging in the importation of slaves at any foreign colony and preventing the outfitting of foreign slave ships in British ports, passed both Houses.

After the recess, Wilberforce worked on his abolition book, which was ready for the press in January 1807. General abolition was now in sight, although Fox, one of its great advocates, had died in June. Prime Minister Grenville, contrary to the usual procedure, decided to introduce an abolitionist measure first in the Lords. Westmoreland railed about "tithes and estates" not being secure, and St. Vincent stormed out of the chamber. Yet by February 10 the bill passed the Lords. The same day the measure was introduced in Commons and passed its first reading.

February 23, the day of the second reading, was one of the finest days in Parliament's history. There was a great expectation of victory as speaker after speaker, rising to advocate abolition and to praise Wilberforce, was greeted with warm applause. Near the end of the night, Sir Samuel Romilly made his now famous contrast between Napoleon and Wilberforce:

*When I look to the man at the head of the French
monarchy, surrounded as he is with all the pomp of
power and all the pride of victory, distributing king-
doms to his family and principalities to his followers, seeming when he sits upon his throne to have
reached the summit of human ambition and the pin-
nacle of earthly happiness—and when I follow that
man into his closet or to his bed, and consider the
pangs with which his solitude must be tortured and
his repose banished, by the recollection of the blood
he has spilled and the oppressions he has committed—and when I compare with those pangs of
remorse the feelings which must accompany my
honourable friend from this House to his home,
after the vote of this night shall have confirmed
the object of his humane and unceasing labours;
when he retires into the bosom of his happy and
delighted family, when he lays himself down on his
bed, reflecting on the innumerable voices that will
be raised in every quarter of the world to bless him,
how much more pure and perfect felicity must he
enjoy, in the consciousness of having preserved so
many millions of his fellow-creatures, than . . .*[76]

At this point, the whole House spontaneously rose
to its feet in a standing ovation, loudly applauding and
wildly cheering Wilberforce. Never before in the history
of Parliament had one of its members received such a
tribute. A tremendous majority, 283 to 16, carried the
bill. By March 25 the bill became law. The long and
arduous struggle had been rewarded. "Oh, what thanks

do I owe the Giver of all good," Wilberforce wrote in his journal, "for bringing me in His gracious providence to this great cause, which at length, after almost nineteen years' labour, is successful!"[77]

Victory had been achieved. Slave trading was now, and forever, legally banished from the British Empire. And this accomplishment marked one of the greatest achievements in human history. As William Lecky has written, "The unweary, unostentatious, and inglorious crusade of England against slavery may probably be regarded as among the three or four perfectly virtuous pages comprised in the history of nations."[78]

# ELDER STATESMAN

*T*HE TRIUMPH OF ABOLITION made Wilberforce a national idol. He had already gained recognition for his *Practical View,* his humanitarian projects, and his independent and principled politics, yet now his moral stature was legendary. He became, in effect, the conscience of the nation. He was recognized and lauded wherever he went. (Not that he lacked detractors; for as we shall see later, both the West Indian planters and the radical Jacobins detested him.)

It was a little surprising, therefore, that so soon after the abolition victory, the 1807 Yorkshire election was contested and Wilberforce had to hit the stump. Despite rumors and lies (such as his premature death) his supporters rallied to his side. As one campaign broadside affirmed:

> *Fame let they trumpet thro Yorkshire resound*
> *And gather the Friends of fair Freedom around;*

> *Unawed by the Great and unbribed by the Court*
> *The pride of our Country shall have our support.*
>
> Chorus
> *Wilberforce is the Man, our Rights to maintain,*
> *The longer we prove him*
> *The better we love him;*
> *We'll support him for Yorkshire again and again.*[79]

Wilberforce won the election but again his health broke down. Indeed, as the years went on, lung trouble (consumption) and curvature of the spine (scoliosis) were added to his constant colitis and weak eyesight. His labors in Commons, of which he was always very conscientious, clearly took their toll on his health.

He was equally conscientious of his duties as a parent. By the end of 1807, he was the father of six children, four boys and two girls. "My children, it is no exaggeration to declare, seldom get a quiet minute with me during the sitting of Parliament," he wrote.[80] He understood that his children had a strong claim on "a father's heart, eye and voice and friendly intercourse."[81] He was especially distressed when one of his children began to cry when he picked him up. The nurse then told Wilberforce that the child "is always afraid of strangers."[82] Thereafter, he sought a better balance between the demands of Westminster and the duties of family. In 1812, he struck a happy bargain: he resigned his seat for Yorkshire and was given the borough of Bramber (a gift of Lord Calthorpe, Barbara's cousin). Now he could stay in public life, without carrying the responsibilities of a major county, while not neglecting his domestic life. Indeed, he loved to spend time with his children, reading to them, taking them to toy shops or the races, or simply playing with them in the yard, garden, or study.

His family notwithstanding, Wilberforce felt that he could not "shut myself up from mankind and immure myself in a cloister. My walk, I am sensible is a public one; my business is in the world; and I must mix in assemblies of men, or quit the post which providence seems to have assigned me."[83] So, from 1807 until his retirement in 1825, he found himself in a whirl of activities and occupations. Both foreign and domestic affairs demanded the utmost attention.

On the foreign front, Napoleon was exiled to Elba, only to return for One Hundred Days of outrage. Not until Waterloo were England and the Continent safe: the Treaty of Vienna was then signed in June of 1815. During the war, however, Anglo-American relations were strained. As early as 1810, Wilberforce had written to John Jay, suggesting that America join Britain in enforcing abolition of the trade, while at the same time expressing fear of future conflict. "Really, the idea of a war between our two countries is perfectly horrible." Yet in 1812 the war came—a war "aggravated by possessing almost the character of civil strife," wrote Wilberforce to Barbara, "a war between two nations, who are children of the same family, and brothers in the same inheritance of human liberty."[84]

The same year that war broke out with America, Wilberforce was working feverishly on a plan to have missionaries sent to India. The charter of the East India Company was up for renewal in 1813, and Wilberforce,

Charles Grant, John Shore, and others rallied public opinion in favor of admitting missionaries to India under the auspices of the British government. Their efforts were rewarded with success.

On the domestic front, scandal and strife consumed Commons. In the early months of 1809, a scandal broke involving the duke of York, George III's second son and commander in chief of the army. It turned out that the duke had kept, and then dismissed, a mistress: a Mrs. Clarke, who was being paid off to keep their former dalliance a secret. When the duke withheld his annual payment, she published letters suggesting that she and the duke had not only had an affair, but that they were both taking bribes from officers in return for promotions. Wilberforce tried to remove the investigation from Commons, and hence from public consumption, because "this melancholy business will do irreparable mischief to public morals, by accustoming the public to hear without emotion of shameless violations of decency."[85] Nevertheless, a public spectacle was made and the duke resigned. Wilberforce was disgusted by the whole ordeal. "It was customary in that house to call things by very soft and gentle names. That which used to be called 'adultery' was now only 'living under the protection.' The rulers of all states," he said quoting Machiavelli, "should take care that religion should be honoured, and all its ceremonies preserved inviolate, for there was not a more certain symptom of the destruction of states, than a contempt for religion and morals."[86]

The royal family also was involved in another prominent scandal. When George III died in January of 1820, his successor, the Prince of Wales, began divorce proceedings against his wife, Caroline. Like so many royal marriages, it was in name only. Each had lived apart and had been guilty of adultery. Despite his own culpability, the prince wanted to remarry, and wanted Caroline stripped of all royal prerogatives. Once more Wilberforce fought a public exhibition, and tried personally to mediate the dispute. Royal pride and arrogance ruined his efforts. The trial proceeded with the Lords in full legal dress. After much unseemly display, the fiasco prematurely ended when Caroline was bought off with a house and fifty thousand pounds a year. She died soon after the coronation.

The economic sacrifices of war and disastrous harvest between 1816 and 1820 made this period one of the most dismal in British history. The lower classes experienced great hardship and deprivation as the standard of living fell. Consequently, there was widespread discontent, which radical agitators flamed by revolutionary rhetoric. In November and December of 1816, the radical Henry "Orator" Hunt organized meetings in Spa Fields, one of which turned into a riot with looting and one murder. Shortly thereafter, bullets shattered the windows of the prince regent's coach. Then, in 1818, sixty thousand people thronged at St. Peter's Fields near Manchester. When the authorities saw that Hunt was there, they marched in to arrest him. The crowd panicked, chaos broke out, and eleven people were killed, with hundreds wounded. "Peterloo," as it was called, brought forth more repression by the government: the Six Acts were swiftly passed through Parliament. Again Wilberforce was placed in the position of having to sacrifice constitutional liberties for his fear of revolution and his hatred of atheism: "[I]t is highly gratifying that all the truly religious classes have nothing to do with the seditious proceedings. The blasphemous songs and papers of the seditious will disgust all who have any religion or any decency."[87]

Wilberforce did what he could on both a professional and personal level to alleviate the suffering of the poor. In 1818 he accompanied Elizabeth Fry to Newgate prison and intervened in a number of cases to save offenders' lives. He voted to lessen the harshness of the penal code. In 1819 he proposed public work projects to aid the working-class poor, and supported a bill to reform child labor and the game laws. He gave generously, out of his own pocket, to those in need, and lowered the rents on the property that he owned. Yet, in spite of these and other efforts by Wilberforce and the Saints, these were bleak years, indeed, in English history.

# The Rattle of Chains

OREMOST AMONG WILBERFORCE'S OCCUPATIONS during this time was the object dearest to his heart—the slaves. On the same day abolition became law, Sierra Leone was turned over to the British Crown. Moreover, Wilberforce and the abolitionists founded the African Institute to expand the work begun there. Its stated objective was "to concert means for improving the opportunity, presented by the abolition of the slave trade, for promoting innocent commerce and civilization in Africa."[88]

It was also now clear that the British law against slave trading was being grossly violated and any successful abolition of the trade would require universal consent. By the end of the long war in Europe, many rulers pledged abolition in their territories: America in 1808, Venezuela in 1810, Sweden in 1812, and Denmark and

Holland in 1814. Spain and Portugal, however, were obdurate. It required British "bribes" to induce them to finally abandon the trade. In a treaty drafted in 1817, Spain agreed to immediate abolition north of the equator, and gradual abolition until 1820 elsewhere. Britain, for her part, agreed to pay the Spanish government 400,000 pounds sterling for compensation. Responding to objections to the treaty in Commons, Wilberforce declared: "Generosity is only justice. Considering the many blessings which the Almighty has showered on this country, it would be shameful to refuse such a sum for so great a purpose."[89] Portugal struck a similar bargain. By 1818, all the powers of the Western world either had implemented abolition or had pledged to do so.

Despite the best efforts of Wilberforce and his fellow Saints in the Commons, illegal smuggling continued. Thus, James Stephen suggested that in order to curtail this illegal activity the West Indian colonies should be required to keep a registry of all slaves in their dominion. The colonies resisted, of course, but eventually agreed—with no real intention of enforcement. As Romilly rightly observed: "Those laws which look so well on paper, which appear so well calculated to benefit the slave population, not only are not executed, but were never intended to be executed."[90] When an uprising occurred in 1816 it was blamed on Wilberforce. "They charge me with fanaticism," he replied. "If to be feelingly alive to the suffering of my fellows is to be a fanatic, I am one of the most incurable fanatics ever permitted to be at large."[91]

In the process of the fight over registration, however, new horror stories drifted back to England. For instance, Commons learned of two slave boys who were each given one hundred lashes for simply stealing a pair of socks. And when their sister, watching the beating, shed sympathetic tears, she was given thirty lashes. Stories such as these were multiplied and convinced Wilberforce that his hope of "amelioration" was a phantom. Only emancipation would end the brutality of slavery. This was in 1818; and Castlereagh warned Wilberforce that, in light of the economic depression at home and the treaty negotiations abroad, he should not press the issue. Wilberforce concurred. Writing to Zachary Macaulay he noted: "We should specially guard against appearing to have a world of our own, and to have little sympathy with the sufferings of our countrymen."[92]

By 1821, Wilberforce's health was collapsing. He was simply too old and frail to undertake the new cause of emancipation. Therefore, in May he approached Thomas Fowell Buxton, a fellow Evangelical and member of Commons. Buxton had Quaker roots and was the brother-in-law of the reformer Elizabeth Fry. Like Wilberforce, he was an independent M.P. and had labored for prison reform. He was bold, daring, and eloquent; and better yet, he was ardent for emancipation. After Buxton had delivered a persuasive speech on capital punishment on May 23, Wilberforce offered him the leadership of the emancipation campaign the next day. Writing from London:

> *Now for many, many years I have been longing*
> *to bring forward that great subject, the condition*

> *of the negro slaves in our Transatlantic colonies,*
> *and the best means of providing for their moral*
> *and social improvement, and ultimately for their*
> *advancement to the rank of a free peasantry—a*
> *cause this, recommended to me, or rather enforced*
> *on me, by every consideration of religion, justice,*
> *and humanity.*
>
> *Under this impression, I have been waiting . . .*
> *for some member of Parliament, who, if I were to*
> *retire, or to be laid by, would be an eligible leader in*
> *this holy enterprise.*
>
> *I have for some time been viewing you in this*
> *connection . . . and can no longer forbear resorting*
> *to you . . . to take most seriously into consideration*
> *the expediency of your devoting yourself to this*
> *blessed service. . . . Let me then entreat you to form*
> *an alliance with me, that may truly be termed holy . . .*
> *; and in forming a* partnership *of this sort with you,*
> *I cannot doubt that I should be doing an act highly*
> *pleasing to God, and beneficial to my fellow-*
> *creatures. . . . If it be His will, may He render you*
> *an instrument of extensive usefulness; but, above*
> *all, may He give you the disposition to say all times,*
> *"Lord, what wouldest thou have me to do, or to*
> *suffer?"*[93]

Such a frank and affectionate appeal could hardly be declined. After some soul-searching, Buxton accepted.

In January of 1822, Wilberforce and others formed the Anti-Slavery Society with the duke of Gloucester as its president, and with five peers and fourteen members of

Parliament among its vice presidents. In July, Wilberforce gave a speech in the Commons urging that slavery be prohibited in the new British settlements in Cape Colony.

> *Let me earnestly conjure the House to estimate this motion at its just importance. . . . And my object is to secure, throughout that vast extent, the prevalence of true British liberty instead of that deadly and destructive evil which would poison the whole body of the soil and render that prodigious area one wide scene of injustice, cruelty and misery. Not only I, but all the chief advocates of the Abolition of the Slave Trade—Mr. Pitt, Mr. Fox, Lord Grenville, Lord Grey and every other—scrupled not to declare from the very first that their object was, by ameliorating regulations and more especially by stopping that influx of uninstructed savages . . . to be surely though slowly advancing towards the period when these unhappy beings might exchange their degraded state of slavery for that of a free and industrious peasantry.*[94]

Despite his growing frailty, it was, according to Buxton, one of the best speeches Wilberforce ever gave. Meanwhile, he was working on another abolition tract, which was published a year later as *Appeal to the Religion, Justice and Humanity of the Inhabitants of the British Empire on Behalf of the Negro Slaves in the West Indies.*

In March of 1823, Wilberforce presented a Quaker petition to Commons requesting it to develop measures to redeem the slaves. In May of the same year, Buxton made a motion "that the state of slavery is repugnant to the principles of the British constitution and of the Christian religion and that it ought to be gradually abolished throughout the British colonies with as much expedition as may be found consistent with a due regard to the well-being of the parties concerned."[95] During the debate, the old worn-out brummagem of revolt was again thrown in the faces of the abolitionists. Wilberforce's reply was direct: "Wherever there is oppression there is danger. . . . The question is how that danger can be avoided. I assume that it is to be avoided by giving liberty for slavery, happiness for misery."[96] Such palpable common sense did not prevail, however. Though certain ameliorative measures were drafted, once again the word *gradual* led to no immediate emancipation.

In the meantime, there was a minor slave uprising in Demarara in which a missionary, John Smith, was falsely charged with fomenting insurrection and left in prison to die. He instantly became the anti-slavery martyr. Wilberforce was indignant at his treatment and death, and despite ill health, returned to Commons in June 1824 to give his last abolition speech in Parliament:

> *It is my daily and nightly prayer—it is the hope and desire I feel from the very bottom of my soul—that so dreadful an event [an uprising] may not occur. But it is a consequence which I cannot but apprehend, and, as an honest man, it is my duty to state that apprehension. Only consider what a terrible thing it is for men who have long lived in a state of*

*darkness, just when the bright beams of day have begun to break in upon their gloom, to have the boon suddenly withdrawn and to be consigned afresh to darkness, uncertainty, nay, to absolute despair! Whatever Parliament may think fit to do, I implore it to do it quickly and firmly. Do not proceed with hesitating steps. Do not tamper with the feelings you have yourselves excited. For hope deferred maketh the heart sick.*[97]

Ten days after the speech, Wilberforce fell critically ill for a month and was forced to rest the remainder of the year. Now he had to face the inevitability of retirement. As was his custom, he made a list of pros and cons. The needs of his family weighed heavily on his mind. As he wrote in a memorandum, "My life is just now peculiarly valuable to my family—all at periods of life and in circumstances which render it extremely desirable . . . that I should be continued to them."[98] Accordingly, as of February 1825, the halls of Commons no longer heard the song of her Nightingale.

# THE MIDNIGHT HOUR

$S$HORTLY AFTER RETIREMENT, Wilberforce moved to Highwood Hill, taking with him his long-standing entourage of servants. Marianne Thornton gives us a vivid picture of his later domestic life: "He has withdrawn from the world with a vengeance, for he is in so little a bit of a House or rather Hutch that some of his servants and most of his guests are sent off to the Inn, a mile away from the house, to sleep." She then described Wilberforce's dependents:

> *Things go on in the old way the house thronged with servants who are all lame or impotent or blind, or kept from charity, an ex-secretary kept because he is grateful, and his wife because she nursed poor Barbara, and an old butler who they wish would not stay but then he is so attached, and his wife who was a cook but now she is so infirm. All this is rather as it should be however for one rather likes*

*to see him so completely in character and would*
*willingly despair of getting one's place changed*
*at dinner and hear a chorus of Bells all day which*
*nobody answers for the sake of seeing Mr. Wilber-*
*force in his element.*[99]

This "scene of happy confusion" was just to Wilberforce's liking, since he did not have the heart to send away
any of his servants and see them suffer. Indeed, his kind
indulgence toward them was a standing joke among his
friends. "Wilberforce has been here with all his household," writes Southey, "and such a household. The principle of the family seems to be that, provided the servants
have faith, good works are not to be expected from them,
and the utter disorder which prevails in consequence is
truly farcical."[100]

During his retirement, he had a settled routine. He
woke at seven, prayed, dressed, listened to his reader,
and had family prayers by nine-thirty. He would then
take a short walk, eat breakfast, and work on correspondence. In late afternoon, he was in the garden with his
reader until dinner at five. The evenings were spent in
conversation, more reading, and prayer. According to
Gurney, "The midnight hour was his zenith, and like
the beautiful Cereus with all her petals extended, he was
then in full bloom."[101]

All of Wilberforce's children were grown by now,
and three of his sons, Robert, Samuel, and Henry,
attended Oriel College, Oxford, and were ordained for
the ministry. The oldest son, William, studied for the
Bar but then decided to undertake dairy farming and a

retail milk business. Wilberforce generously allowed William to farm his land and invested heavily in the scheme. William invested his inheritance and borrowed from several other sources. Unfortunately, the venture ended in disaster: William had incurred as much as fifty thousand pounds (two million of today's dollars) in debt. Wilberforce, in order to save his son from ruin, chose to shoulder the debt himself by selling all his properties. After 1830, he had no permanent place to lay his head. Upon leaving Highwood he repined: "What I shall miss most is my books and my garden, though I own I do feel a little for not being able to ask my friends to take a dinner or bed with me, under my own roof."[102] He spent the last few years of his life staying with either Robert or Samuel.

Although he was out of politics and public life, Wilberforce stayed abreast of the abolition movement. In 1830 he made his last appearance in the chair of the Anti-Slavery Society, where he paid a touching tribute to his old fellow-soldier Clarkson. The Reform Bill passed Parliament in June of 1832, and the first reformed Parliament returned a large number of abolitionists.

In April of 1833, Wilberforce was persuaded to make one last public appearance for the cause that had engaged his entire political career. At Maidstone he made a speech offering a petition against slavery. His body and voice were worn with age but the old fire still burned. "I trust that we now approach the very end or our career," he concluded. And at that moment a shaft of sunlight rushed into the room. Seizing the omen, Wilberforce exclaimed, "The object is bright before us, the light of heaven beams upon it, and is an earnest of our success."[103] The speech was prophetic, for the end of Wilberforce's career and the end of slavery coincided.

By July he was totally broken in health, yet he bore his dissolution with dignity. He was now, he told a friend, "like a clock which is almost run down."[104] On the twenty-fifth, the young William Gladstone, future prime minister, paid Wilberforce a visit. "He is cheerful and serene," he observed in his diary, "a beautiful picture of old age in sight of immortality. Heard him pray with his family. Blessing and honour are upon his head."[105]

The next day, a bill for the Abolition of Slavery passed its third reading in Commons. "He exulted in the success," wrote the younger Macaulay, who had visited Wilberforce the following day.[106] That was on Saturday. On the next night he was drifting into glory. By Monday morning, July 29, 1833, Wilberforce, the champion of freedom, was free from this mortal clay.

When news reached London, Brougham, as Lord Chancellor, sent an address to Wilberforce's sons requesting that burial be made in Westminster Abbey. This was an unprecedented honor for a private individual without rank or title. Both Houses suspended business to attend a funeral thronged with mourners. Appropriately, Wilberforce was laid to rest near the tombs of Pitt and Fox.

# TRIBUTE

*A*YEAR AFTER HIS DEATH a statue of Wilberforce was erected in the north aisle of Westminster Abbey. The epitaph, penned by Macaulay, beautifully summa-rizes the greatness of Wilberforce's character and life:

*TO THE MEMORY OF*

## William Wilberforce

(BORN IN HULL AUGUST 24TH 1759,
DIED IN LONDON JULY 29TH 1833)
FOR NEARLY HALF A CENTURY A MEMBER OF THE HOUSE OF COMMONS,
AND, FOR SIX PARLIAMENTS DURING THAT PERIOD,
ONE OF THE TWO REPRESENTATIVES FOR YORKSHIRE.

IN AN AGE AND COUNTRY FERTILE IN GREAT AND GOOD MEN,
HE WAS AMONG THE FOREMOST OF THOSE WHO FIXED THE
CHARACTER OF THEIR TIMES
BECAUSE TO HIGH AND VARIOUS TALENTS
TO WARM BENEVOLENCE, AND TO UNIVERSAL CANDOUR,
HE ADDED THE ABIDING ELOQUENCE OF A CHRISTIAN LIFE.

EMINENT AS HE WAS IN EVERY DEPARTMENT OF PUBLIC LABOUR,
AND A LEADER IN EVERY WORK OF CHARITY,
WHETHER TO RELIEVE THE TEMPORAL OR THE SPIRITUAL WANTS OF HIS
FELLOW MEN
HIS NAME WILL EVER BE SPECIALLY IDENTIFIED
WITH THOSE EXERTIONS
WHICH, BY THE BLESSING OF GOD, REMOVED FROM ENGLAND
THE GUILT OF THE AFRICAN SLAVE TRADE,
AND PREPARED THE WAY FOR THE ABOLITION OF SLAVERY
IN EVERY COLONY OF THE EMPIRE:

IN THE PROSECUTION OF THESE OBJECTS,
HE RELIED, NOT IN VAIN, ON GOD;
BUT IN THE PROGRESS, HE WAS CALLED TO ENDURE
GREAT OBLOQUY AND GREAT OPPOSITION:
HE OUTLIVED, HOWEVER, ALL ENMITY:
AND, IN THE EVENING OF HIS DAYS,
WITHDREW FROM PUBLIC LIFE AND PUBLIC OBSERVATION
TO THE BOSOM OF HIS FAMILY.
YET HE DIED NOT UNNOTICED OR FORGOTTEN BY HIS COUNTRY:
THE PEERS AND COMMONS OF ENGLAND,
WITH THE LORD CHANCELLOR, AND THE SPEAKER, AT THEIR HEAD,
CARRIED HIM TO HIS FITTING PLACE
AMOUNG THE MIGHTY DEAD AROUND,

HERE TO REPOSE:
TILL, THROUGH THE MERITS OF JESUS CHRIST,
HIS ONLY REDEEMER AND SAVIOUR,
(WHOM, IN HIS LIFE AND IN HIS WRITINGS HE HAD DESIRED TO GLORIFY),
HE SHALL RISE IN THE RESURRECTION OF THE JUST.[107]

# PART II
## THE CHARACTER OF
### WILLIAM WILBERFORCE

*The picture which the dead leave on the minds of their survivors is not always lively or distinct, but no one who has been accustomed to observe Wilberforce will ever find the slightest difficulty in picturing him on the tablet of the mind.*[1]

*Wilberforce, sir, is a little creature; he is an ugly creature; but look in his face, hear him speak, you forget it all; he is the incarnation of love.*[2]

*I am aware that while writing of William Wilberforce one must appear to use continually the language of panegyric; but the real fact is, that his was not only a very extraordinary, but a very lovely character, and one of which the faults were not likely to be put on record for posterity.*[3]

# PROVIDENCE

*How much do they lose of comfort, as well as,*
*I believe, in incentives to gratitude and love . . .*
*who do not accustom themselves to watch the*
*operations of the Divine Hand.*[4]

NY ATTEMPT TO INTERPRET THE WAYS of Providence
is a daring enterprise. Yet it is striking to observe
the number of events that occur in a leader's life which
serve either to prepare him for leadership or to further
the objectives laid before him. This is the inscrutable element in leadership. And it is amply illustrated in the life
of Wilberforce.

Even before his birth, Providence was setting the
stage for his career in politics. His grandfather and father
had labored successfully as merchants and amassed a
small fortune. He additionally had familial connections

with the Thorntons, who were also prosperous. With the death of his father, and then his uncle, Wilberforce became independently wealthy and had the luxury of pursuing Parliament. His good family name and abundant fortune aided his successful bid for Hull. After finding his political calling, his financial capital served as a war chest to fund many of his humanitarian projects.

It was certainly no coincidence that Wilberforce asked Milner to accompany him on those fateful tours in 1784–85. He could have invited any number of people. Nevertheless, by happenstance (from the human point of view) he asked Milner, a man who was religiously qualified to lead him to Christ. But "had I known," he later wrote, "what his religious opinions were, it would have decided me against making the offer; so true is it that a gracious hand leads us in ways that we know not, and blesses us not only without, but even against our own plans and inclinations."[5] And then there was the fortuitous appearance of Doddridge's book, which Wilberforce just "happened" to pick up. Reflecting later on this conversion, Wilberforce saw the workings of Providence: "How much it depended on contingencies! If he [Milner] had been ill as he was afterwards or if I had known his character, we should not have gone together. . . . Doddridge's *Rise and Progress* having fallen in my way so providentially whilst abroad. . . ."[6]

But the workings of Providence were not limited to purely "spiritual" matters like conversion. Wilberforce believed that his political career was a manifestation of Providence also. His bid for the great seat of Yorkshire, when a political no-name, was, upon reflection, a mad scheme; and his subsequent victory could only be ascribed to Providence:

> *I had formed within my own heart the project of standing for the county [York]. To any one besides myself I was aware that it must appear so mad a scheme that I never mentioned it to Mr. Pitt, or any of my political connexions. It was undoubtedly a bold idea, but I was then very ambitious. However, entertaining it, I carefully prepared myself for the public debate, which was soon to follow in the face of the whole county; and both at the public meeting and in the subsequent discussions, it was this idea which regulated the line, as well as animated the spirit of my exertions. All circumstances, indeed, considered . . . my mercantile origin, my want of connexion or acquaintance with any of the nobility or gentry of Yorkshire . . . my being elected for that great county appears to me, upon the retrospect, so utterly improbable, that I cannot but ascribe it to a providential intimation that the idea of my attaining that high honour suggested itself to my imagination, and, in fact fixed itself within my mind.[7]*

Briefly after his conversion, Wilberforce was tempted to withdraw from politics; but after much thought he realized that Providence had placed him there. Writing to his mother he said: "What I have said will, I hope, be sufficient to remove any apprehensions that I mean to shut myself up either in my closet in town, or in my heritage in the country. No, my dear mother, in my circumstances this would merit no better name than desertion; and if I were thus to fly from the post where Providence has placed me, I know not how I could look for the blessing of God upon my retirement. . . ."[8] "I must mix in the assemblies of men or quit the post which Providence seems to have assigned me."[9]

Just as Wilberforce was preparing to embark on the long abolition campaign he fell seriously ill. The best doctor of the day declared his case hopeless. Miraculously he survived. Writing to his son Samuel many years later, he saw his recovery and long life as another sign of Providence: "And yet, as I think, I must have told you, Dr. Warren, the first medical authority of that day, declared in 1788 that I could not then last above two or three weeks, not so much from the violence of an illness from which I had then suffered, as from the utter want of stamina. Yet a gracious Providence has not only spared my life, but permitted me to see several of my dear children advancing into life. . . ."[10]

Providence, according to Wilberforce, worked on a national scale as well as a personal scale. God governed the affairs of nations, and could even use a tyrant like Napoleon. "This man," he wrote in 1808, "is manifestly an instrument in the hands of Providence; when God has done with him, He will probably show how easily He can get rid of him. Meanwhile may we be of the number of those who trust in Him, and all will be well." After Napoleon's return from exile, Wilberforce wrote to his son: "Able, and active, and wicked as Buonaparte is, he is no less under the Divine control than the weakest of human beings."[11]

Whether contemplating the smallest fact of nature or the grandest fate of nations, Wilberforce sought to behold the hand of God. That was the key to his patience and perseverance. Likewise, it kept him humble. He realized that his great success in the cause of abolition was more than the work of his hand alone. An invisible Hand had also been at work. "Surely it calls for deep humiliation and warm acknowledgment," he wrote soon after his victory in 1807, "that God has given me favour with men; that, after guiding me by His providence to that great cause, He crowned my efforts with success. . . ."[12]

# Religion

*This is the very perfection of religion; "Whether we eat or drink or whatever we do, do all to the glory of God."*[13]

*W*ILBERFORCE'S VIEW OF PROVIDENCE was the result of the religious worldview that he adopted after his conversion. Before then, he had imbibed the fashionable skepticism of the upper classes.

Indeed, the upper classes were for the most part either nominal Christians or outright pagans. The bright-burning candle of religious fervor that pervaded England during the seventeenth century, as evidenced by the ministries of such worthies as Bunyan or Hooker, was nearly extinguished. By the turn of the century, Deism had become the ruling theology of the Established Church. Biblical Christianity was under assault, which called forth the defensive efforts of some able apolo-

gists: Isaac Newton produced his *Fulfilled Prophecies,*
Nathaniel Lardner his *Credibility of the Gospel History,*
and Bishop Butler his *Analogy*—yet all to no avail. There
was at the time, said Archbishop Secker, "an open disre-
gard for religion," and Butler lamented that "it had come
. . . to be taken for granted by many that Christianity
had been at length discovered to be fictitious, and that
nothing remained but to set it up as a principal subject of
mirth and ridicule."[14]

Churches were nearly empty and true religion nearly
extinct. Contemporaries like Addison asserted that there
was less religion in England than any neighboring country, while Montesquieu declared that there was no religion in England at all. Historians such as Canon Ryle
stated that "duelling, adultery, fornication, gambling,
swearing, Sabbath-breaking, and drunkenness were
hardly regarded as vices at all. They were the fashionable
practices of people in the highest ranks of society."[15]

Then came the Great Awakening a few decades
before Wilberforce's birth—first with Whitefield, then
with the Wesley brothers, and then with a small army of
evangelical preachers like Rowland, Grimshaw, Fletcher,
Romaine, and others. There was a great quickening.
Thousands were converted. Yet the greatest labor was
done outside the Established Church and among the
lower classes. The Awakening notwithstanding, during
Wilberforce's lifetime, observed one biographer, "the
Church had lapsed into a state of near paganism."[16] The
well-known philosopher and churchman Bishop Berke-
ley confessed: "In these times a cold indifference for the
national religion—indeed, for all matters of faith and

Divine worship—is thought good sense." He added: "It is even become fashionable to deny religion; and that little talent of ridicule is applied to such wrong purposes that a good Christian can hardly keep himself in countenance."[17] Wilberforce's dear friend Hannah More wrote in 1787, "Those who are able to make a fair comparison must allow that, however the present age may be improved in other important and valuable advantages, yet there is but little appearance remaining among the great and the powerful of that righteousness that exalteth a nation."[18]

Torpor and unbelief overwhelmed many of the established clergy. Upon hearing the best preachers in London, the great jurist Blackstone declared that "not one of the sermons contained more Christianity than the writings of Cicero." And the ever-perceptive Samuel Johnson once confided to Boswell that he had never met a religious clergyman.[19] While the city clergy patronized the rich and influential, the rural clergy abandoned their flocks. As late as 1812, nearly three-fifths of the country clergy were nonresident. Of those who remained many were either boorish or scandalous.[20] Except for Henry Rider, who was made bishop of Gloucester in 1815, no evangelical clergyman received an English diocese until 1827, when Wilberforce's cousin Charles Sumner was granted Winchester.

Though Wilberforce remained attached to the Established Church, he was part of the evangelical wing, the Anglican mirror of the Methodist revival. He repudiated the skepticism of his pre-conversion days and accepted the cardinal doctrines of Christianity. He believed in the trinity of the Godhead, the deity and virgin birth of Christ, the depravity of man, the blood atonement, salvation by grace through faith, the future bliss of the righteous, and the damnation of the unrighteous. Not that these doctrines were peculiar to Wilberforce or the Evangelicals; they were not. The real difference was that Wilberforce and his fellow Saints really believed them—and acted on them. They had experienced the new birth and strove to walk in a vital relationship with God. They believed that true Christianity was a comprehensive worldview. As biographer Furneaux has noted: "Their main theme was that it was not enough for a man to be a 'nominal Christian,' to conform to Christianity, to avoid breaking any of the Commandments, to go to Church on Sunday and then to forget about God for the rest of the week. Christianity should instead be carried into every corner of life and allowed to fill it."[21]

One of the best comprehensive descriptions of Wilberforce's Evangelicalism is given by historian S. C. Carpenter:

> The Evangelicals brought to bear on the life of England an intense belief in God and in the saving power of the Christian Gospel, an intense belief in the necessity of personal conversion, and an intense moral earnestness. Their own lives were strictly ordered. Every hour, every shilling belonged to God. They prayed, they worked, they gave alms, they performed their deeds of charity with scrupulous devotion, living all their lives "in the great Taskmaster's eye." They read and studied the Bible uncritically,

*as was inevitable, but with unwearying zeal. They
observed Sunday with strictness, and their hymns
gave a new popularity and a new brightness to the
service of the Church. They assembled their house-
holds for family prayers, they published religious
literature which had a wide circulation, and they
brought about a great improvement in the language
and habits of many whose deeper selves they could
not touch. Marriage, which had been cheapened
in the previous century, was restored to something
like its proper credit. They did not cover all the
ground, because there were not very many of them,
and there were some matters which their limited
range did not enable them to reach, but they were
in deadly earnest, and wherever their influence penetrated at all it penetrated very deep.*[22]

The key word here is *earnestness.* Wilberforce took
his faith seriously, and what he put his hand to do, he did
to the glory of God and the good of mankind: "Such was
the religion of Wilberforce—not a cold, abstract belief in
dogmas, but a life of ungrudging, fervent, loving activity,
a life given up to the service of men."[23] It was this seriousness and zeal that made him not only a godly Christian but also a great leader.

# Integrity

*In short, . . . the best preparation for being a good politician, as well as a superior man in every other line, is to be a truly religious person. . . . Whatever is to be the effect of subordinate machinery, the main-spring must be the desire to please God . . . and an aspiration after increasing holiness of heart and life.*[24]

*P*OLITICIANS COMMONLY MAKE public professions of piety. They want to be trusted, of course, so what better way than by appearing moral and religious. But are these professions genuine or are they a public façade? Does the man practice in private what he preaches in public? Since true leadership entails integrity, what a leader says and does must be one.

That was certainly the case with Wilberforce. His views on true Christian conduct were well publicized in his *Practical View*. Indeed, the main goal of the book, he wrote, was "not to convince the Sceptic, or to answer the arguments of persons who avowedly oppose the fundamental doctrines of our Religion; but to point out the scanty and erroneous system of the bulk of those who belong to the class of orthodox Christians. . . ."[25] The "erroneous system" was not just doctrinal misunderstanding; it was also the failure to live according to what was professed. For many in the upper and middle classes of society their Christian profession was a façade and their church attendance a charade.

Wilberforce, on the contrary, strove to practice in private the Christian disciplines that he so strenuously advocated in public. "The most malicious cynic," said historian Coupland, "could not accuse the author of the *Practical View* of failing to practice what he preached."[26] He gave up gaming, dancing, and the theater not only because they were associated with immorality, but because they dulled the mind to spiritual things and were a simple waste of time—time that could be spent in devotions. "Oh, what folly!" he would write in his diary after a social outing. "What forgetfulness of God!"[27]

Beginning in 1794, Wilberforce started a new journal in which to keep track of his spiritual growth, particularly his attempts to gain victory over what he considered his besetting sins. Each page had a heading like "volatility," "wandering in prayer," "humility," "truth erring," or some such title. For the next six years he privately cataloged his battle against sin and his quest for holiness. A typical journal entry of the time reads:

*July 15, 1795 — The result of examination shows me that though my deliberate plans are formed in the fear of God, and with reference to His will, yet that when I go into company (on which I resolve as pleasing to God) I am apt to forget Him; my serious-ness flies away; the temptations of the moment to vanity and volatility get the better of me. If I have any misgivings at the time they are a sullen, low grumbling of conscience, which is disregarded. Although, therefore, I am not defective in external duties to God, or grossly towards my fellow-creatures, but rather the contrary, yet I seem to want a larger measure, first, of that true faith that realizes unseen things, and produces seriousness; and, second, of that vigour of the religious affec-tions, which by making communion with God and Christ through the Spirit more fervent and habitual, might render me apt and alert to spiritual things.*[28]

Journal entries such as this one could be multiplied ad infinitum. Yet, they speak less of Wilberforce's failure than of his earnest desire after holiness and Christ. To this end, he spent many hours in private prayer and medita-tion. Shortly after the triumph of abolition, he reflected: "How little also have I borne in mind that we are to be strangers and pilgrims on the earth! This impression can be kept up in those who are in such a state of prosperity and comfort as myself, by much prayer and meditation, and by striving habitually to walk by faith, and to have my conversation in heaven."[29]

Wilberforce was naturally gregarious. He loved dining and conversation. He was allured by the temporal pleasures of fashionable society. He could easily immerse himself in the constant whirl of business and social life. He enjoyed the wit, the banter, the foining. That was his social side—a side free of any gross or scandalous conduct. But the private side—the side where Wilberforce engaged in fastidious self-examination—is where we see his true integrity. He took great pains to be not merely a nominal Christian but an authentic Christian. As he wrote to his cousin Mary Bird in 1789:

> The genuine Christian strives not to prove himself guiltless but humbles himself in the dust and acknowledges that he is not worthy of the least of all God's mercies. He takes a survey of his past life and of the state of his temper and affection; these he compares with the law of God and contrasts with the bounty and longsuffering, etc. of his Creator and is ready to despair, when he reads the gracious invitation: Come unto Me all ye that labour and are heavy-laden and I will give you rest, and he reads, God so loved the world that he gave his only-begotten Son, etc. This revives his hopes, but heightens his shame and self-abhorrence. His language is "Oh that I might therefore show myself in some sort worthy of this infinite love, infinite condescension and unutterable love."[30]

Whatever his venial shortcomings, Wilberforce had the virtue of integrity. He only asked of others what he himself was willing to do. He practiced what he preached. By doing so he gained the respect that pays tribute to moral authority, that fundamental requirement of leadership.

# FAULTS

*Faults he has, as who is free from them?*[31]

*N*O ONE EXPECTS A LEADER TO BE PERFECT. It is enough that he is good. A virtuous character does not imply perfection; rather, it suggests a character in which high and noble habits predominate and moral defects are under control, though not necessarily eliminated. What Wilberforce said of Pitt could be said of any leader, including himself: "Faults he has, as who is free from them?"

One of Wilberforce's nagging faults was his "butterfly mind." His attention was easily diverted from important business by trivial or urgent interruptions. While discussing the fate of African slaves with Stephen or Babington, he could the next moment be found throwing flowers at Marianne Thornton or crawling on the floor for marbles.

In conversation he quite naturally flitted from one subject to another with no apparent rhyme or reason; his madness appeared to have no method: "When I look into my mind I find it a perfect chaos, wherein the little knowledge which I do possess is but confusedly and darkly visible."[32]

Though this trait could be exasperating to such grave friends as James Stephen or Zachary Macaulay, to others it was part of his endearing charm. Wilberforce, however, saw it as a fault that lent to a waste of time. Consequently, in the winter of 1788 he tried to develop a more systematic use of his time by charting how he spent every hour of each day.

Wilberforce could also be guilty of indecision and procrastination. His speeches were often marked with tangents and digressions that demonstrated an annoying knack for seeing both sides of a question. After years of parliamentary speaking, it became a standing joke that you could "predict his vote, for it was certain to be opposed to his speech."[33] His procrastination equally sprang from the same source. He would often agonize over a decision and make a memorandum listing pros and cons. While struggling with the question of registration in the West Indies, he wrote the following note: "Against precipitancy—Moses eighty, Aaron eighty-three years old when God sent them to lead out the Israelites from Egypt. Abrahm one hundred years old when Isaac born. Our Saviour himself 30 years old before he came forth, having till then probably worked with his father at his trade."[34] However, once his mind was made up, he was tenacious and persevering, as the entire abolition struggle shows.

James Stephen could be brutally frank in pointing out Wilberforce's faults. Once, when urging Wilberforce to retire his Yorkshire seat, he wrote to him: "A man has no right to be a husband and a father unless he will give to those relations an adequate part of his time." At another time he pointed out what many saw as Wilberforce's chief fault. Critiquing one of his abolition speeches, he said: "Your great defect has always been want of preparation in cases that demand it, and—with those who do not know your habits—raise the expectation of it. No man does so little justice to his own powers. That you stand so high as you do is because you could stand much higher if you would—that is, if you could and would take time to arrange your matter."[35]

One mark of Wilberforce's greatness was his willingness to receive the criticism of Stephen and others. Instead of defending himself or retaliating, he heard their reproofs with thoughtful, and even thankful, candor. On one occasion, after being rebuked by Stephen, Wilberforce wrote to him:

> *Go on, my dear Sir, and welcome. Believe me, I wish you not to abate anything of the force or frankness of your animadversions. . . . For your frankness I feel myself obliged. Openness is the only foundation and preservative of friendship. . . . Let me therefore claim from you at all times your undisguised opinions.*[36]

Writing to his daughter Lizzy, Wilberforce observed that telling a friend his faults was the "best prerogative" and "the most sacred and indispensable duty of friendship." And as he told Samuel, being reproved by one's friends is, though unpleasant at first, a great blessing:

> It is a great pleasure to me that you wish to know your faults. Even if we are a little nettled when we first hear of them, especially when they are such as we thought we were free from, or such as we are ashamed that others should discover, yet if we soon recover our good-humour, and treat with kindness the person who has told us of them, it is a very good sign. It may help us to do this to reflect that such persons are rendering us, even when they themselves may not mean it, but may even only be gratifying their own dislike of us, the greatest almost of all services, perhaps may be helping us to obtain an eternal increase of our happiness and glory.[37]

Wilberforce had the wisdom to see his shortcomings, the humility to admit them, and the will to fight against them. He was a great leader, not because he was perfect, but because he readily acknowledged his faults and was willing to correct them.

# Self-Improvement

*The degrees of happiness and glory which He
will grant to us will be proportioned to the
degree of holiness we have obtained, the degree
(in other words) in which we have improved the
talents committed to our stewardship.* [38]

*W*ILBERFORCE WAS ONE OF THOSE rare reformers
who actually lived by the dictum "Reformation begins at home." Though legislating for reform was
critical, he apparently understood that the best way to
change the world was to fix one soul at a time—including
his own. While working for the reformation of manners,
the abolition of the slave trade, the reform of Parliament,
and the general improvement of societal conditions, he
also labored at that all-important task of leadership, self-
improvement.

As noted previously, Wilberforce practiced rigorous self-inspection. Throughout his entire life he kept journals and examined himself on almost a daily basis. On the Sabbath, which he observed religiously, he took special time to evaluate his spiritual and moral condition. He was also concerned about wasting time when he had so many important tasks before him. Writing to his son in 1822 he said:

> *I cannot today send you the account of time, but I will transmit it to you. It was a very simple business, and the chief object was to take precautions against the disposition to waste time at breakfast and other rendezvous, which I have found in myself when with agreeable companions, and to prove to myself by the decisive test of figures that I was not working so hard as I should have supposed from a general survey of my day. The grand point is to maintain an habitual sense of responsibility and to practise self-examination daily as to the past and the future day.*[39]

Wilberforce realized that, due to his "sober dissipation" during his college days, he was sorely unfit for the leadership to which God had called him. He forever regretted that he had idled away his years at Cambridge as a dilettante. Writing later he noted:

> *But those with whom I was intimate did not act towards me the part of Christians, or even of honest men. Their object seemed to be to make and keep me idle. If ever I appeared studious, they would*

> *say to me, "Why in the world should a man of your future trouble himself with fagging?" I was a good classic and acquitted myself well in the College examinations; but mathematics, which my mind greatly needed, I almost entirely neglected, and was told I was far too clever to require them. Whilst my companions were reading hard and attending lectures, card parties and idle amusements consumed my time. The tutors would often say within my hearing, that "They were mere saps, but that I did all by talent." This was poison to a mind constituted like mine.*[40]

Though it sounds as if he is blaming others, Wilberforce accepted responsibility for his laziness, recognizing that he had been duped by his own vanity. He had no one to blame but himself.

Accordingly, he set about to make up for lost time and to improve his store of knowledge. He learned the true value of time and began a program of systematic study and reading. From shortly after his conversion to his marriage twenty years later, he spent two months every summer in reclusive study. In 1797 he noted in his diary how to best use his summer recess for self-improvement: "The recess for six weeks is commencing. I once meant to try to finish my tract, but I now rather think that, the time being too little for so very serious work, I shall devote it to preparation for the house of Commons—improvement in speaking, which sadly neglected, and in knowledge."[41]

He began to devour the classics, history, philosophy, poetry, economics, politics, and theology. He read
Montesquieu, Blackstone, Adam Smith, John Locke, and
Alexander Pope. He reveled in Cowper and Samuel Johnson. His favorite book was, of course, the Bible, which
he read incessantly. Historian Seeley accurately describes
both the painful fact and positive fruit of Wilberforce's
intellectual self-improvement:

> *Fully recognizing the peculiar sphere in which he
> was called to do his life-work, William Wilberforce
> at once, and in the first place, set himself to the
> apportioning of his time, and to the acquisition
> of regular habits, more especially in the matter
> of study. It was difficult for him, with his large
> acquaintance and public duties, to find the quiet
> that he wished; but he set himself to read, and that
> with such a right good will, not in one line only,
> but in every branch of literature which he felt to
> be useful—from light to heavy and heavy to light,
> and so his mind soon came to be a storehouse of
> knowledge. Keeping up this habit, too, from youth
> to age, with only the sight of one eye, and when, to
> use up the odds and ends of time, he had to employ
> a reader to attend him while dressing, he was really
> au fait in most subjects, and in a position to form a
> judgment on most questions.*[42]

One question that Wilberforce had to master was
the question of slavery and the trade. Immediately after
taking up the mantle of abolition, for instance, he settled

down at Thomas Gisborne's Yoxall Lodge during the summer and began to intensively master the subject by collecting information and marshaling his facts. He and Thomas Babington spent nearly nine and a half hours each day engrossed in their preparation for debate. The scene is described by another friend who was there:

> *Mr. Wilberforce and Mr. Babington have never appeared downstairs since we came, except to take a hasty dinner, and for half an hour after we have supped; the slave trade now occupies them nine hours daily. . . . They talk of sitting up one night in each week to accomplish their task. The two friends begin to look very ill, but they are in excellent spirits. . . . Mr. Wilberforce is now never riotous and noisy, but very cheerful, sometimes lively, but talks a good deal more on serious subjects than he used to do. Food, beyond what is absolutely necessary for his existence, seems quite given up.*[43]

Wilberforce's quest for self-improvement—excellence in character and talents—paid off. He won the most important battles of his long career: the trade was abolished, the slaves were emancipated, and society was improved. More important, he paid the price to become the world-class leader God had called him to be.

# Books

*I feel most the separation from my books.*[44]

I T SOUNDS TRITE TO SAY THAT A LEADER must be a reader. Yet it is one of those truisms that happen to be true. Ignorance is never a virtue, especially in a leader. If a man is going to command the respect of his followers he must be their superior in wisdom and knowledge. While there is much to be said for the wisdom that comes through experience, there is a vast sea of knowledge that can be traversed only by rowing the oars of a good library.

Throughout his adult life Wilberforce was an avid reader and lover of books. In addition to any special reading he undertook for his parliamentary projects, he enjoyed a wide range of literature, poetry, history, and theology. James Stephen, who knew Wilberforce intimately, said that "a man of more varied reading or better taste will seldom be found."[45] His reading, however, was eclectic: "an ill-sorted and heterogeneous mess, made up of history, morals, philosophy, poetry, statistics, ephemeral politics and Theology, all in turn either lightly scanned, or diligently studied. . . . He would controvert, interrogate, or applaud in the form of marginal notes, when he was alone, or, if an auditor was at hand, in spoken comments. . . ."[46] Consider this diary entry from 1807:

> *Paley's Natural Theology, Adam Smith, popular pamphlets, Bisanquet's Value of Commerce— clever, but rash, and in parts unfair, but not designedly; a man should always have a friend to run over his writings—Cobbett too, and Edinburgh Review, and Eclectic; Mrs. Hutchinson's Memoirs of Colonel H.—beautiful; Spence against Foreign Commerce—sad stuff, a vile mingle mangle of blundering conclusions from Adam Smith, Economists, etc.; Lowe on State of West Indies—oil without vinegar; Concessions of America the Bane of Great Britain; excellent critique on Malthus in Christian Observer, which Bowdler's I am sure; Lay of Last Minstrel, Looking over East India Documents for civilizing and converting natives, Buchanan's Ecclesiastical Establishment, and Wrangham's Civilization of Hindoos.*[47]

He loved to read while taking walks, and if with a friend, he would read out loud. Indeed, Wilberforce was a veritable walking library. He cherished his books so much that he had his suits specially tailored with extra pockets in which to carry his portable tomes. His friend

John Harford related how "we were often amused by the capacity of his pockets, which carried a greater number of books than would seem, if enumerated, possible, and his local memory was such that, on drawing out any author, he seemed instantaneously to light on the passage which he wanted."[48]

Wilberforce had a great fondness for poetry. Cowper, the author of "The Negro's Complaint," was undoubtedly his favorite poet, for both his literary and moral excellence. "His piety," he wrote in 1809, "gives unfading charms to his compositions." He read, and several times met, the poet Wordsworth. The poems of Sir Walter Scott he highly admired, but he was less fond of Scott's novels. As literature, he recognized the high merit of Scott's works, but Wilberforce felt that the moral element was lacking. What he said of *The Lady of the Lake* sums up his view aptly: "Really I did not think that I continued in such a degree subject to the fascination of poetry. I have been absolutely bewitched. I could not keep the imaginary personages out of my mind when I most wished to remove them. How wonderful is this dominion over the heart which genius exercises! There are some parts of the poem that are quite inimitable. . . . I regret there not being so much of moral as in Marmion." In addition, he cherished Shakespeare—which he read aloud in the evenings—Milton, Dryden, Southey, Mason, and Rogers. The classic poets also charmed him. Virgil he tried to read daily, and Horace he annotated and memorized.[49]

History captivated Wilberforce, and on one occasion he and Babington were so engrossed with reading English history that they took the book with them on their daily walks, "one of them reading aloud whilst his steps were guided by the other."[50] Of the ancient historians Thucydides was his favorite. Concerning his famous contemporary Gibbon, he said: "He is an extraordinary man. Coxcomb all over, but of great learning as well as very great show of it. He has the merit also of never declining a difficulty. But his style is abominably affected, and perfectly corresponds with Lord Sheffield's account of his mode of composition, and then his paganism is vastly more confirmed than that of Tully, or any other of the old school."[51]

Wilberforce's reading included some of the church's great divines, such as Doddridge, Richard Baxter, and John Owen, whose work "On Spiritual Mindedness" he strongly recommended. The Bible he studied (not just read) daily; and when time permitted he would study it hours on end and memorize long passages.[52]

While Wilberforce enjoyed reading and literature for its entertainment and instruction, he tried to turn everything that he learned to good use. Whether writing exhortatory letters, dispensing witty conversation or delivering a parliamentary speech, his store of knowledge served him well. As Buxton has rightly observed: "His taste for books was not that of a student who becomes absorbed in study for its own sake, but rather that of one who reads for the sake of the matter to be found in books, to be stored up and turned to good account in due time."[53] He learned from his books, said Stephen, "to understand, and so to benefit, mankind."[54]

This is a lesson every leader should learn: to be studious but not pedantic, knowledgeable but not doctrinaire. He gains from his reading more than facts; he gains wisdom, an essential element of sound leadership.

# CHARM

*We ought to be always making it our endeavour
to be experiencing peace and joy in believing,
and that we do not enjoy more of this sunshine
of the breast is, I fear, almost always our own
fault.*[55]

CHARM IS ONE OF THOSE INTANGIBLE QUALITIES easy to recognize but difficult to define. Like the wind, which blows where it wills, it is more felt than seen.

All those who met Wilberforce were enchanted by the effects of his charm. Over and over we hear of the light, the sunshine, the warmth of his presence. We hear of his humor, his wit, his mimicry. We learn of his storytelling and singing. We are told of the peace and serenity he exuded. In spite of his hectic pace and solemn obligations, he seemed to be always riding the crest of a rolling wave. He was energetic but not frantic; earnest but not churlish. His was a heat that warms but does not burn, a lamp that lightens but does not blind.

It was Wilberforce's charm that gave him entrance to London's luxurious clubs. He was amusing and had a keen sense of the ludicrous. One night when he and some friends were "clubbing," someone happened to eulogize a pretty girl named Barbara St. John. Wilberforce immediately spun his own silly doggerel:

> *And if you continue to torture us*
> *You are no longer Barbara but barbarous.*[56]

Wilberforce's singing voice was so good that the Prince of Wales once told the duchess of Devonshire that he would go anywhere to hear Wilberforce sing. On one occasion, as George Selwyn was leaving Commons, he observed Wilberforce and the "gang" foining. They "made me, for their life and spirit, wish for one night to be twenty. There was a table full of them drinking—young Pitt, Lord Euston, Barkley, North, etc. etc. staging and laughing *à gorge deployée*. Some of them sang very good catches: one Wilberforce, a M. P., sang the best."[57]

After his conversion Wilberforce quit the clubs but was still conspicuously sociable and even more charming than before. Though he might still engage in repartee and turn a bon mot, his conversation was now more elevated, instructive, and edifying. He avoided the vulgar but was not a prude. He had what Lord Milton described as "the close union between the most rigid principles and the most gay and playful disposition." Maria Edgeworth met Wilberforce in 1821 and described him as follows:

*I cannot tell you how glad I am to have met him
again, and to have had an opportunity of hearing
his delightful conversation. . . . He is not at all
anxious to merely talk. His thoughts flow in such
abundance, and from so many sources, that they
often cross one another. . . . As he literally seems
to speak all his thoughts as they occur, he produces
what strikes him on both sides of any question. This
often puzzles his hearers, but to me it is a proof of
candour and sincerity; and it is both amusing and
instructive to see him thus balancing accounts out
loud. He is very lively and full of odd contortions:
no matter. His indulgent, benevolent temper strikes
one particularly: he makes no pretension to superior
sanctity or strictness.*[58]

Sir James Mackintosh, a radical freethinker, noted Wilberforce's charm: "If I were called upon to describe Wilberforce in one word, I should say he was the most 'amusable' man I ever met with in my life. Instead of having to think what subject will interest him, it is perfectly impossible to hit on one that does not. I never saw any one who touched on life at so many points; and this is the more remarkable in a man who is supposed to live absorbed in the contemplation of a future state."[59]

Describing a typical conversation over breakfast, Stephen recalled "the same simple-hearted, natural man, talking without effort or preparation or disguise from the overflowing of his mind." Wilberforce's humor, he observed, was not "one terse and pregnant jest: he rather used it as a toy to be tossed about and played with for a while, and then thrown aside. . . . Being himself amused and interested by everything, whatever he said became amusing or interesting. . . . His mirth was as exhilarating as the first laughter of childhood."[60]

Speaking of childhood, Marianne Thornton tells of Wilberforce's love for children and her own playful inter-action with him when she was a small child. As "grave discussion" went on between Wilberforce, her father, and others, Wilberforce "was most thankful to refresh himself by throwing a ball or a bunch of flowers at me, or opening the glass door and going off with me for a race on the lawn." One of her first lessons had been "never disturb Papa when he was talking or reading. . . ." Wilberforce was another matter: "No such prohibition existed with Mr. Wilberforce. His love for, and enjoy-ment in, all children was remarkable."[61]

In 1814 the well-known French author Madame de Staël was in London, and the one man she most wanted to meet was Wilberforce. She used Sir Romilly as a mes-senger and persuaded Wilberforce to attend one of her extravagant soirees. It was "a cheerful, pleasant dinner," he noted in his diary. "A brilliant assembly of rank and talent." Madame de Staël was delighted with Wilber-force, exclaiming to Mackintosh, "Wilberforce is the best converser I have met with in this country. I have always heard that he was the most religious, but I now find that he is the wittiest man in England."[62] Such opinions of Wilberforce were shared by most who met him.

Even those prejudiced against him often found his charm winsome. Immediately after the abolition vic-tory, the saints were celebrating at Palace Yard. Reginald Heber, a High Churchman and later bishop of Calcutta, was present and met Wilberforce for the first time. Although he had previously been prejudiced against Evangelicalism, after meeting Wilberforce he told a friend, "How an hour's conversation can dissolve the prejudice of years!"[63]

Wilberforce's charm was a key ingredient in his success. He was not one of those reformers who shuffled about with furrowed brow, muttering curses at the world's injustice; or who railed at authorities while sowing "the dragon's teeth of moral indignation."[64] Rather, he disarmed his enemies with charming kindness, and he won adherents to his causes by being winsome himself—a rare accomplishment for any reformer.

# FRIENDSHIP

*Oh remember, my dearest boy, to form
friendships with those only who love and serve
God, and when once you have formed them,
then preserve them as the most valuable of all
possessions.*[65]

O NE INDISPENSABLE TRAIT of a first-class leader is his
ability to develop and maintain sound friendships.
Since a man's friends shape his thought and life, it is
imperative to choose one's friends wisely. A leader must
remember the proverb: "The wise walk with the wise,
but the companion of fools becomes base."[66]

While a mere lad of twelve, Wilberforce wrote a preco-
cious essay on friendship, which is worth quoting at length
since it lays out principles that guided him throughout life:

*Nothing gives a greater tincture to the Mind or Morals of Man than either the good or bad Qualities possessed by those with whom they associate. A Person by being very intimate with another and being constantly in his Company naturally imbibes his Manners, and the same Sentiments occur to him; which tho' perhaps they may be in some Measure wrong yet having the Sanction of a friend it is very likely that they will be winked at and overlooked.*

*In nothing is there a greater difference than in a good or a bad Companion whether one considers it in regard to his Morals or Understanding. A real good Companion is not one who can sit over so many Bottles, or play so many pools at Quadrille; but one whom Good Sense, Good-Nature and good education and improved understanding have all conspired to render truly agreeable. He must in his behaviour be free and open without Plasticity, genteel and complaisant without flattery. He must not affect to appear ignorant of what he really knows or fond of displaying his Superior Knowledge. . . . A person possessed of these Qualifications may be called a truly good Companion, and it is amazing the effect which the company of such a person may produce. On the contrary a Companion unworthy of the name in a manner rusts and corrodes every one with whom he is intimate. Since there is so much to be got by the Society of a good Companion and as much to be lost by that of a bad one we ought to take the greatest care not to form any improper connections. . . .*[67]

Wilberforce never wavered from these principles. At St. John's he avoided the more vulgar students, associating rather with men like Eliot and Gisborne. Later, he met William Pitt, with whom he struck up an intimate, lifelong friendship. Pitt was really the ideal friend: he was, in Wilberforce's view, the very paragon of intellectual and moral virtue. Writing a "Sketch of Pitt" years after his death, Wilberforce lauded his "extraordinary intellectual and moral powers. . . ." There was a "clearness of his conceptions" and "there never was a fairer reasoner." Pitt also had an "extraordinary memory" and "considerable powers of imagination and much ready wit. . . ." He had "great natural courage and fortitude" combined with a "naturally sanguine temper. . . ." He possessed "good humour and candour. . . . In society he was remarkably cheerful and pleasant, full of wit and playfulness. . . ." Most notably for Wilberforce, Pitt's "regard for truth was greater than I ever saw in any man who was not strongly under the influence of a powerful principle of religion: he appeared to adhere to it out of respect to himself, from a certain moral purity which appeared to be a part of his nature." Pitt was equally a man of "public spirit and patriotism"—"no man, I believe, ever loved his country with a warmer or more sincere affection. . . ."[68]

The one thing that Pitt lacked was the "principle of religion." He was not a Christian like Wilberforce, and this fact was a hindrance to their intimacy on the deepest level. Nevertheless, they remained close friends until Pitt's death.

Other than Pitt, Wilberforce's best associates were all believers. He surrounded himself not only with good men but with godly men. As he wrote to his son Samuel: "Oh remember, my dearest boy, to form friendships with those only who love and serve God, and when once you have formed them, then preserve them as the most valuable of all possessions."[69] Wilberforce did this himself. And the result was the formation of a community of believers known as the Saints, or Clapham Sect: Thornton, Venn, Bankes, Sharp, Clarkson, both Macaulays, Hannah More, and many, many others. They prayed together, worshiped together, supported one another, and even reproved one another in love. Each had undergone conversion and was "pledged not only to the great causes they undertook together, but also to help their friends attain the character and destiny which God revealed for them."[70]

The impact of Wilberforce on his friends is illustrated by the testimony of Henry Thornton:

> *Few men have been blessed with worthier or better friends than have fallen to my lot. Mr. Wilberforce stands at the head of these, for he was the friend of my youth. I owed much to him in every sense, soon after I came out in life; for his enlarged mind, his affectionate and condescending manners, his very superior piety, were exactly calculated to supply what was wanting to my improvement and my establishment in a right course. It is chiefly through him that I have been introduced to a variety of other most valuable associates. When I entered life I saw a great deal of dishonourable conduct among people who made great profession of religion. In my*

*father's house I met with persons of this sort. This
so disgusted me that, had it not been for the admi-
rable pattern of consistency and disinterestedness
which I saw in Mr. Wilberforce, I should have been
in danger of a sort of infidelity.*[71]

Wilberforce was so likable that, when it came to
friends, he could have picked the choicest fruit of society's garden. Yet he was not seduced by the forbidden
tree. He understood the Proverbial saying "iron that
sharpens iron, so does a man the countenance of his
friends." Therefore, a leader must choose his friends
with caution, as did Wilberforce, and use the power of
friendship to expand his influence for good.

# TEAMWORK

*No man has perhaps more cause for gratitude to God than myself. But of all the various instances of His goodness, the greatest of all, excepting only His Heavenly Grace, is the many kind friends with whom a Gracious Providence has blessed me.*[72]

*W*HETHER IT IS CALLED TEAM-BUILDING or networking, a leader must have the capacity to attract to himself disparate individuals and to mold them into a committed and hard-working team. He must have, as Wilberforce described it, "a gravitational force."

This gift was a chief mark of Wilberforce's leadership. Indeed, without the dedication and labor of a small group of like-minded friends, he never would have achieved his lifelong ambition of abolishing slavery in the British Empire. As biographer Garth Lean has noted, Wilberforce needed his friends "to make him what he was, but they needed him to transform their many interests into a river of reform."[73] In addition to his many other talents, it was Wilberforce's genius for friendship that enabled him to make such a profound impact on Parliament and the nation of England. Like many other great leaders, Wilberforce never worked alone, and from his first days in politics he labored in tandem with a group of reformers known as "the Saints."

Chief among them was Henry Thornton, who was a close personal friend and fellow member of Parliament. The two had met at the home of Thornton's father, who lived in Clapham. And it was there that Wilberforce and Thornton, in 1792, lived together as bachelors in a house purchased by Wilberforce. Later, when each married, they stayed neighbors on the same estate in Clapham, and "the Saints," or "Clapham Sect," began to gather around them. Thornton was a successful banker like his father before him, and possessed both a keen mind for abstract economics and a sound business sense. Thus it was no surprise that when the Saints planned any of their many social reforms they turned to Henry for practical business advice and financial support.[74]

Granville Sharp, a brilliant and eccentric scholar, was another of the group, and the one who originally recruited Wilberforce to the cause of abolition. It was Sharp who, in 1772, undertook the case of a beaten and abandoned slave, and secured the famous ruling that essentially declared that any slave who set foot in English territory must be considered free. Thus, he single-handedly overturned the legal opinion of the most renowned jurists in England. Later, Sharp was the Saint who initiated the Sierra Leone project, which was designed to provide a home in Africa for any freed slaves who desired to return there.

The "chaplain" of the Clapham Sect was John Venn, the rector of the parish church in Clapham. Besides providing spiritual guidance to the group, Venn collaborated with them and led many of their causes. He started a system of parish visitation, founded the Society for Bettering the Condition of the Poor, and was the prime mover behind the national Church Missionary Society, which he founded in 1799.

Hannah More, one of the many women associated with Clapham, was a determined religious activist—so determined that it earned her the title "petticoat bishop." A successful poet and playwright, More had hobnobbed in the fashionable intellectual circle of London, claiming David Garrick and Samuel Johnson as friends. However, after a conversion or rededication in the 1780s, More began a career as an educator and writer on behalf of the lower classes, helping to organize schools for the poor. She likewise used her pen to provide inexpensive reading material for the disadvantaged. Her Cheap Repository Tracts, as they were called, sold for a penny apiece, and were underwritten by Thornton. Within a year after publication, more than two million had been sold.[75]

Whenever Wilberforce, Thornton, or any other member of the Saints needed a fact or figure, they often quipped, "Look it up in Macaulay!"—Zachary Macaulay, that is, the group's one-man research department. Indeed, Macaulay's photographic memory, tireless research, and incisive analysis made his reports so reliable that "it became a dictum that Macaulay could be quoted on the floor of the House of Commons without fear of contradiction."[76] After serving as governor of Sierra Leone for six years, Macaulay became, in 1802, the first editor of the *Christian Observer.* He was additionally a member of twenty-three philanthropic and religious societies, and sat on the board of nine.

The list of Wilberforce's "Saints" could be expanded to include such notables as James Stephen, Charles Grant, and Thomas Clarkson (one of the most important but less appreciated of British abolitionists), Thomas Babington, and many others. But one thing is certain: despite their varied talents, their effectiveness as a team was a result of Wilberforce's vision, plus that intangible atmosphere that flowed from his optimism, charm, and friendship. "On the whole I am in hopes some good may come out of Clapham system," wrote Thornton. "Mr. Wilberforce is a candle that should not be hid under a bushel. The influence of his conversation is great and striking."[77] Like other great leaders, the force of Wilberforce's personality drew men together and mobilized their energies for a greater good.

# CHARITY

*A vigorous principle of enlarged and active
charity springs up within us; and we go forth
with alacrity, desirous of treading in the steps
of our blessed Master, and of manifesting our
gratitude for his unmerited goodness, by bearing
each other's burdens, and abounding in the
disinterested labors of benevolence.*[78]

ALL THE POLITICAL CLAPTRAP about compassion and
tolerance notwithstanding, it is interesting to
note that the cardinal virtue of charity means love for
God, and only secondarily, love for our fellow man.
Indeed, that is always the proper order. For if we pre-
sume to love men before God then we fall into the
idolatry of humanism: worshiping the creature above
the Creator. Yet when God has his rightful place in
our minds and hearts, then we are bound—indeed,
we are moved—to show genuine charity toward our

neighbor. Being heavenly minded we accomplish much earthly good.

William Wilberforce was a compassionate politician because he was first and foremost a Christian statesman. After his conversion in 1784–85, he felt that God himself had issued to him a divine call to oppose slavery and to attempt a reformation of morality in England. In both crusades he was motivated and sustained by the inner charity or love for God that was the hidden spring of all his actions, both public and private. In essence, his entire political career was the expression of his belief in the efficacy of practical Christianity.

Even while fighting the colossal struggle against slavery, Wilberforce never forgot his second great object, the "reformation of manners"—that is, his attempt to elevate the moral condition of British society. This he hoped to accomplish, first, by "suppressing vice," and second, by educating the upper classes on the true nature of Christianity.

Admittedly, pre-Victorian England was in need of reformation. The middle and upper classes were for the most part engrossed in splendid vices: luxurious extravagance, haughty insouciance, and rank venality. Drunkenness and adultery were common and acceptable. As historian John Marlowe points out:

> The venality of English political life was the counterpart of the coarseness and profligacy of the social life of the English governing classes. And there was a quality about it even more repellent than venal-

*ity—the quality of heartlessness. There was very little
to choose between the political and social morals of
the English and the French aristocracy in the century
before the French revolution.*[79]

Their moral condition was succinctly summarized
by Furneaux: "The rich lived in a state of selfish pagan
hedonism."[80]

Many in the lower classes fared little better, despite
Wesley's revival, due to their brutal working conditions.
Men, women, and children labored in foul, fetid factories for up to sixteen hours a day, six days a week.
Women suffered and sweated in dark, dank coal mines,
while their young children toiled from dawn till dusk in
the colliers. Many of the poor were degraded and sottish,
drowning in a sea of gin; some destitute mothers even
killed their children to sell their clothes for gin money.
Law and order decayed. The government's only response
was to extend the death penalty to such minor offenses
as stealing a rabbit or cutting down a tree.

Wilberforce's task of reformation, therefore, was a
formidable one. Yet when George III issued the traditional (but perfunctory) "Proclamation for the Encouragement of Piety and Virtue and for the Preventing of
Vice, Profaneness and Immorality," Wilberforce set to
work. He established a Proclamation Society, comprised
of some of Britain's most prominent leaders, designed to
see that the royal proclamation became "a force rather
than a farce."[81] Meanwhile, Hannah More began to write
and distribute her cheap tracts to reach the lower classes
with the message of morality and Christianity.

Wilberforce himself also took up his pen and aimed it at the upper classes. In 1797, he published his *Practical View,* the aim of which is suggested by its long original title: *A Practical View of the Prevailing Religious System of Professed Christians in the Higher and Middle Classes iContrasted with Real Christianity.* His publisher, Thomas Cadell, was skeptical that a religious book by a politician would sell, and suggested that only five hundred copies be printed. Much to his surprise, the book became an instant bestseller. Nearly eight thousand copies (in five editions) were sold in six months, and by 1826, it had gone through more editions and been translated into French, Italian, Dutch, and German. In England, many of the upper classes read the book and were converted.

"Good causes," observes biographer Pollock, "attached themselves to Wilberforce like pins to a magnet."[82] Indeed they did; for the range of his philanthropic projects is breathtaking. In addition to the abolition movement and the Proclamation Society, Wilberforce and the Saints worked for reparations to Africa, missionaries for India, the establishment of Sunday schools in the Mendips and elsewhere, the Society for the Bettering of the Poor, the Church Missionary Society, the British and Foreign Bible Society, and many more smaller organizations. At one time, Wilberforce was a contributor to sixty-nine organizations, the patron of one, the vice president of twenty-nine, the treasurer of one, the governor of five, and a committee member of five. Moreover, he fought to improve working conditions for the poor, protested the game laws, and legislated to reform child labor laws and the penal code.

At the heart of Wilberforce's crusades was Christ. And it was Christ who was at the center of the Clapham Sect. The success of the Saints was rooted in their assurance that their sins were forgiven in Christ. "They knew," writes Roger Anstey, "not only that they could overcome evil in their own hearts but also that they could conquer the evils in the world which they felt called to combat."[83]

Understanding the true nature of charity, Wilberforce and his friends sought to love God supremely while serving their fellow men sacrificially. Genuine charity, contrary to either a sentimental tolerance or indifferent pietism, was born of spiritual devotion and resulted in social action. "Faith worketh by love."[84]

# BENEVOLENCE

*The great rule practically for pleasing our*
*Saviour in all the little events of the day is to*
*be thinking of Him occasionally and trying to*
*please Him, by not merely not doing evil, but by*
*doing good; not merely negatively trying not*
*to be unkind, not to be disobedient, not to give*
*pain, but trying positively, to be kind, to be*
*obedient, to give pleasure.*[85]

*U*NLIKE SO MUCH MODERN WELFARE, Wilberforce's elee-
mosynary enterprises were neither political bribes
nor public masquerades. He was not buying votes, nor
was he running a continuous campaign. Rather, he actually cared for people. As one visitor put it, he breathed "a
spirit of general benevolence."[86]

So great was Wilberforce's kindness that it became
proverbial: it seemed that nearly everyone who knew

him could tell a story illustrating his concern for others. For instance, Patty More (the lesser-known sister of Hannah More), tells of Wilberforce's first visit to their cottage at Cowslip Green, in the Cheddar region. The cliffs of Cheddar were renowned, and Patty hoped that Wilberforce would be impressed with their beauty. She was rather surprised, and humbled, by his response. Instead of marveling at these adamantine attractions, he pondered the plight of the poor who languished under their shadows. As Patty relates:

> *The cliffs of Cheddar are esteemed the greatest curiosity in these parts. We recommended Mr. W. not to quit the country till he had spent a day in surveying these tremendous works of nature. . . . He went. I was in the parlour when he returned. With the eagerness of vanity, having recommended the pleasure, I inquired how he liked the cliffs. He replied, they were very fine; but the poverty and distress of the people were dreadful. . . . I said to his sister and mine that I feared Mr. W. was not well. The cold chicken and wine, put into the carriage for his dinner, were returned untouched. Mr. W. returned at supper, seemingly refreshed with a higher feast that we had sent with him. The servant, at his desire, was dismissed, when immediately he began, "Miss Hannah More, something must be done for Cheddar." He then proceeded to a particular account of his day,—of the inquiries he had made respecting the poor. There was no resident ministry, no manufactory, nor did there appear any*

*dawn of comfort either in their spiritual or temporal condition. The method or possibility of assisting them was discussed till a late hour; it was at length decided in a few words by Mr. W.'s exclaiming, "If you will be at the trouble, I will be at the expense." We turned many schemes in our heads, in every possible way; at length those measures were adopted which led to the foundation of the different schools.[87]*

Lord Clarendon tells a story of how Wilberforce allowed himself to be pulled away from important parliamentary business so he might attend to the needs of a poor stranger:

*I was with him once when he was preparing an important notion in the House of Commons. While he was most deeply engaged, a poor man called, I think his name was Simkins, who was in danger of being imprisoned for a small debt. Wilberforce did not like to become his security without inquiry; it was contrary to a rule he had made but nothing could induce him to send the man away. "His goods," said he, "will be seized and the poor fellow will be totally ruined." I believe at last he paid the debt himself; but remember well the interruption which it gave to his business, which he would not resume till the case was provided for.[88]*

Wilberforce's sympathetic and generous ear was always open to the cries of the needy. In the years before his marriage, he gave away anywhere from a third to a quarter of his income; and after marriage he continued to be sacrificially generous. He gave personal gifts whenever he heard of a need. Often, the money was distributed through an intermediary: a clergyman would be given an annual gift to be distributed to the poor in his parish, or a friend would be asked to pass along a contribution anonymously. Other times, Wilberforce would visit a debtor's prison with his "hand in his pocket." In 1801, the Napoleonic wars and calamitous harvest led to great hardship for the poor. Wilberforce worked feverishly for their relief, trying to persuade the government to grant some public funds, while he himself sent his own money to friends in Yorkshire, asking them to disperse it to the poor. In that year alone, he gave away three thousand pounds beyond his income.

Moreover, he sat as the governor of St. Bartholomew's Hospital, starting in 1788, after having sent a large donation. He encouraged the founding of Samaritan Societies to care for the poor who were discharged from charity hospitals, like St. George's. He assisted destitute orphans, such as Gordon Smith, who later became an army doctor. He supported the Elland Society, which trained young men for the ministry, and he personally paid for tutors to prepare certain young men for college. The Bettering Society, whose mission was the "scientific investigation of the problems of poverty, and the circulation of information about methods of relief and improvements of living conditions," and which founded many hospitals, was actually started in Wilberforce's home four days before Christmas of 1796.

Wilberforce was once described as a "Minister of Public Charity." Indeed, he was, but even more impressive was his private charity. "He was not the sort of hypocrite who preaches philanthropy all day, then goes home and bullies his dependents at night."[89] Private acts of kindness, however small, more reveal a man's character than public claims of charity, however large. The proof of Wilberforce's sincerity is all that he gave, both in time and treasure, out of the public eye. "Do not your alms before men" was the rule that governed his benevolence.

# INDUSTRY

*Christianity calls her professors to a state of
diligent watchfulness and active services. But
the persons of whom we are now speaking,
forgetting alike the duties they owe to themselves
and to their fellow-creatures, often act as though
their condition were meant to be a state of
uniform indulgence, and vacant, unprofitable
sloth.*[90]

*O*NE FEATURE COMMON TO ALL great leaders is their
large capacity for work. Their noteworthy accomplishments are a direct result of the amount of time and
energy directed toward their goal. Conviction must give
birth to action. Good intentions or noble sentiments
mean little without old-fashioned industry.

Wilberforce often complained that one of his greatest
faults was his "want of application." According to his son

Samuel, "He said he thought the habit of such importance that he would willingly consent to give up all his present knowledge. That he should not know one word even of Latin—that his whole memory of times past should be one universal blank; if at that price he could procure for himself the power of applying his mind to the employment in which he was engaged instead of sitting an hour over his work without giving ten minutes really to it." He likewise complained that his mind was not as clear and sharp as needed in order to tackle his work: "When I look into my mind I do find it a perfect chaos, wherein the little knowledge which I do possess is but confusedly and darkly visible."[91]

While these statements are probably exaggerations (Wilberforce was notoriously critical of himself), it was undoubtedly true that he had to constantly fight against his "butterfly" mind and natural indolence. These flaws were exacerbated, moreover, by his medicinal use of opium, which tends to depress the nervous system. At the same time, Wilberforce's spider-web mind was part of what made him so entertaining, adding to his charm.

Whatever his natural tendencies, Wilberforce understood the value of work and arduously labored for the causes in which he believed. He was not an armchair philanthropist. He was a toiler. For instance, when he first undertook the cause of abolition, he labored incessantly in early 1789 to prepare for his maiden speech: "Jan. 26: House near six, slave business all evening, with only biscuit and wine and water." In February he noted: "Slave business till near bed, and slept ill. . . ." Again the same month: "On full conviction from experience that it is impossible for me to make myself master of the slave subject and to go through my various occupations except I live more undistractedly, I determine scarce ever to dine out in parties, and in all respects to live with a view to those great matters till the slave business is brought to some conclusion. May God bless the work and my endeavour."[92]

Over a year later, Wilberforce and Babington spent between nine and ten hours a day studying the slave trade in preparation for the upcoming fight in Commons. His diary reveals the strain: "Oct. 8: Unwell. Hard work—slave evidence. Oct. 9: Eyes bad. Hard at work. Oct. 11: Slave evidence, and very hard at it with Babington all this week: wherein by God's blessing enabled to preserve a better sense of heavenly things than for some time before. Nov. 1: Continued to work very hard at evidence all this week. Slept ill, not being well, partly through working too much."[93] The campaign for abolition was to last another seventeen years.

But abolition was not Wilberforce's only cause. His many other humanitarian designs brought added labor. He had meetings to attend, speeches to give, charities to support, prisons to visit, and on and on.

When at home he was inundated with a constant stream of petitioners of all stripes seeking his aid or advice. His anteroom swelled with an odd mixture of suppliants: "On one chair sat a Yorkshire constituent, manufacturing or agricultural; on another a petitioner for charity of a House of Commons client; on another a Wesleyan preacher; while side by side with an African, a foreign missionary, or a Haytian professor, sat perhaps some man of rank who sought a private interview and whose name had accidentally escaped announcement."[94] On one occasion a woman simply burst into his home and exclaimed, "Mr. Wilberforce I have run away." Scenes like these were common, which is why Hannah More succinctly described his home as "Noah's Ark, full of beasts, clean and unclean."[95]

In 1808 Wilberforce moved from Broomfield to Kensington Gore and bought a secret house next door, which he called "the Nuisance." This was his polite way of trying to attend to business and avoid the overwhelming number of uninvited guests. The only problem was that because of his scrupulous honesty he would not let his footman tell intruders he was out, for that would encourage him to lie.

Wilberforce also had to face stacks of correspondence. He often received thirty letters a day for many days in a row. Since he did not like to use an amanuensis, he would spend hours on end answering every letter himself, which put a terrible strain on his already weak eyesight. His regular correspondents were friends like Hannah More, John Newton, Isaac Milner, Thomas Gisborne, and many others. Plus he had official correspondence with dignitaries: emperors, kings, presidents, and bishops. And then there was the fixed flow of unsolicited letters asking for help, advice, or favors: Clarkson wanted a professorship for himself; Simeon wanted an honorary degree for his brother; and Lady Caroline Lamb wanted him to visit her son's sick friend.

It is true that Wilberforce did not have the power of systematic and continuous labor, as did such friends as

Clarkson or Stephen. Yet he made up for it by a sympathetic assiduity for all who were suffering. Milner's depic-
tion of Wilberforce's labor for the poor during 1800–1801
could serve as an epitaph for his entire life:

> *Our dear and benevolent friend absolutely*
> *exhausted his strength on this subject. He is the*
> *most feeling soul I ever knew; and also the most*
> *patient and indefatigable in endeavouring to lessen*
> *the miseries of the people: and how he does get*
> *misrepresented and abused! But you may kick him*
> *as long and as much as you please; if he could but*
> *fill the bellies of the poor, he would willingly submit*
> *to it all.*[96]

# Sabbath

*Let us appeal to the Day which is especially
devoted to the offices of Religion: do they joyfully
avail themselves of this blessed opportunity of
withdrawing from the business and cares of life;
when, without being disquieted by any doubt
whether they are not neglecting the duties of
their proper callings, they may be allowed to
detach their minds from earthly things, that by a
fuller knowledge of heavenly objects, and a more
habitual acquaintance with them, their hope may
grow more "full of immortality"?* [97]

IT WAS ONCE MENTIONED OF MOZART that his genius lay
not only in how he scored his notes but also where he
placed his rests. The same could be said for Wilberforce.
His daily toil for men was punctuated by his weekly rest
in God. The two were, in fact, inseparable; for it was his
Sunday rest that refreshed and strengthened him for a

lifelong commitment to good works.

Throughout his life (that is, after his conversion) Wilberforce regularly and religiously observed the Sabbath. It was his rule never to conduct business on Sunday, and only once or twice in his long career did he ever violate that rule. His custom was to spend the day alone, if possible, or to invite a friend, or two, who "likes our way of going on, upon that day."

A typical Sabbath began with family prayers, breakfast, and then morning church. Then Wilberforce, either alone or perhaps with a friend, would take a leisurely and contemplative stroll before the three o'clock dinner. After dinner any guests were left to themselves as Wilberforce would spend the next hour and a half in private devotions. "I almost seem at this moment," recalled Dr. Harford, "to behold him on one of these occasions passing through the anteroom of his library, when about thus to retire, with a folio under his arm, and stopping me with a smile to tell me that his companion was a volume of Baxter's Works." These devotions were followed by evening church, then supper, and finally either edifying conversation or the reading of poetry by Wilberforce.[98]

The Sabbath was not, as many thought, a dreary day of boredom. "The Sunday is with them," wrote Wilberforce, "to say the best of it, a heavy day; and that larger part of it which is not claimed by the public offices of church, dully drawls on in comfortless vacuity, or without improvements, is trifled away in vain and unprofitable discourse."[99] On the contrary, the Sabbath was a day for religious exercises and spiritual refreshment. It was a day of joy and thanksgiving—a time to recall one's blessing and to offer praise to God. It was a day of meditation and reflection—a time to renew the mind and to set the affections on heavenly realities. It was a day of public worship and corporate fellowship. It was, at least for Wilberforce, a spiritual feast.

In his *Practical View,* he laid out just how the Sabbath ought to be employed. Challenging the nonobservance of the upper classes, he says:

> *Is the day cheerfully devoted to those holy exercises for which it was appointed? Do they indeed "come into the courts of God with gladness"? And how are they employed when not engaged in the public services of the day? Are they busied in studying the word of God, in meditating on his perfections, in tracing his providential dispensations, in admiring his works, in revolving his mercies (above all, the transcendent mercies of redeeming love), in singing his praises, "and speaking good of his name"? Do their secret retirements witness the earnestness of their prayers and the warmth of their thanksgivings, their diligence and impartiality in the necessary work of self-examination, their mindfulness of the benevolent duty of intercession? Is the kind purpose of the institution of a Sabbath answered by them, in its being made to their servants and dependents a season of rest and comfort? Does the instruction of their families, or of the more poor and ignorant of their neighbors, possess its due share of their time?*[100]

Though Wilberforce believed that the observance of the Sabbath was a duty, he viewed it more as a privilege and a blessing—a spiritual day of rest that brought many benefits.

> *It might be deemed a privilege thus to spend it, in the more immediate presence of our Heavenly Father, in the exercises of humble admiration and grateful homage; of the benevolent and domestic, and social feelings, and of all the best affections of our nature, prompted by their true motives, conversant about their proper objects, and directed their noblest end; all sorrows mitigated, all cares suspended, all fears repressed, every angry emotion softened, every envious or revengeful, or malignant passion expelled; and the bosom, this quieted, purified, enlarged, ennobled, partaking almost of a measure of the Heavenly happiness, and become for a while the seat of love, and joy, and confidence, and harmony.*[101]

The truth of his notions was painfully brought home when Wilberforce learned of the suicide of Castlereagh in August of 1822. Writing to Stephen he says,

> *It is very curious to hear the newspapers speaking of incessant application to business, forgetting that by the weekly admission of a day of rest, which our Maker has graciously enjoined, our faculties would be preserved from the effects of this constant strain. I am strongly impressed by the recollection of your*

*endeavour to prevail on the lawyers to give up
Sunday consultations in which poor Romilly would
not concur. If he had suffered his mind to enjoy
such occasional remissions, it is highly probable the
strings would never have snapped as they did from
over-tension.*[102]

Wilberforce wished to disperse the benefits of the
Sabbath throughout society. The Proclamation Society
tried to encourage the observance of Sunday, and Wilberforce attempted to have official entertainment moved to
Saturday. He asked Speaker Addington to move his levees
to Saturday, and he persuaded Perceval, when prime minister, to move the reassembling of Parliament to Tuesday
instead of Monday, so travel would not be necessary on
the Sabbath. In 1798, he supported the veto of a bill that
would have made military drilling compulsory on the Sabbath; and in 1799 he, along with Lord Pelgrave and Pitt,
promoted a bill (which failed) to ban Sunday newspapers.

Due to his personal efforts and example, the observance of the Sabbath became much more common—in
fact, somewhat fashionable, by the end of the eighteenth
century. And the Victorian observance has been traced to
Wilberforce's influence.

More significantly, it was his own observance of the
Sabbath that provided the refreshment and strength he
needed to persevere in his myriad campaigns. As Coupland has judiciously observed, Wilberforce's Sabbath
exercises "braced him for the business of the active world
outside." This "chronic invalid" was enabled to "fight
down fatigue, to work as hard, day in, day out, as most

stronger men; to brush aside the worry of hostility and insult; to hold up, year after year, often almost single-handed, the drooping banner of his cause; and finally to achieve as great a thing as any of his great contemporaries achieved for the good name of his country and the welfare of mankind."[103]

This is quite a tribute, not only to Wilberforce, but also to the value of the Sabbath.

# EVANGELISM

*What a comfort it is to know that our Heavenly Father is ever ready to receive all who call upon Him.*[104]

*W*ILBERFORCE'S SABBATH EXERCISES were designed to give him temporary relief from his worldly cares. Yet one care he never let go, even on the Sabbath, was his care for the souls of men. He had undergone the new birth, and he desired others to experience the same enriching and ennobling experience. So, while his *Practical View* did its work on a national level, Wilberforce did his work as a fisher of men on a individual level.

He took personal witnessing seriously and kept a "Friends' Paper" in his Bible. Next to the names of thirty of his friends, he jotted down ideas for how, when talking with them, he could lead casual conversation into deeper religious discussion. These "launchers," as he called them, were designed to help each of his friends take a closer step to receiving Christ. Every Sunday, Wilberforce would take the list out of his Bible, review it, revise it, and pray over it.

The following sample from his "Friends' Paper" is dated January 12, 1794, and has the instruction "to be looked at every Sunday":

> *S_____ and Mrs. What books reading? To give them good ones—Walker's Sermons. Call on Mrs. S and talk a little. Lend her Venn's last Sermon. Education of their children, to inquire about. Prayer, etc. Their coming some Sunday to Battersea Rise to hear Venn. Call often, and be kind.*
>
> *Lady A_____ and Sir R. Has he read Doddridge? Be open to her, etc.*
>
> *Mr. And Mrs. M_____. Encourage to family prayers, etc.*
>
> *Lord and Lady T_____. See them. Get at them through G_____. Discover what books reading.*
>
> *V_____. Try what he believes and speak home truths.*
>
> *The T_____s. Call and sound them on religion. Give them money to give away, etc. Little presents.*
>
> *Lady E_____. Speak pretty openly, yet tenderly.*[105]

Wilberforce would often agonize over his friends in prayer, spending hours contemplating the best "launcher" appropriate for each. When in society he was amiable as ever, yet always looking for opportune moments to turn the conversation toward religion. Commonly, "when I have appeared gay and unthinking," he wrote, "I have been secretly influenced by a desire of promoting their dearest interests."[106] Sometimes he might merely mention a good book or simply assure someone of his prayers.

In many cases his "launchers" worked, with Wilberforce making many converts. When Edward Eliot lost his wife (Pitt's sister) a few days after giving birth to a daughter in September 1786, Wilberforce was there to console him and lead him to Christ. "It pleased God to draw me," wrote Eliot, "by the bereavement to a better mind." Eliot became one of his dearest friends in Parliament. "Pray for me, my dear friend, as I do for you," he wrote Eliot. "We can render each other no more effectual service." In 1788 when Lord Muncaster lost his young son and heir, Wilberforce wrote an affectionate evangelistic note. "I take up my pen instinctively, yet what can I say but recommend you to the tender mercies of our Heavenly Father who in all his chastisements has a gracious meaning and who has promised that all shall work together for good to them that love him. Oh, Muncaster, He so loved the world that he gave his only begotten son to die for us. . . ."[107]

The papers of other friends such as Lord Apsley, Henry Addington, and Lord Belgrave show Wilberforce's efforts to convert them. Another friend, Matthew Montagu, and his wife, actually laughed at Wilberforce when he suggested saying grace before meals. Yet by 1790 Wilberforce was writing to Montagu as a fellow believer, requesting to be remembered "at the Throne of Grace."

Wilberforce also won his sister to Christ, and his mother became progressively more religious as she got older.

Some friends were unyielding, however. Lord Carrington (Bob Smith) proudly asserted, "He knew he could never convert me." (Although Wilberforce did win Smith's daughters to Christ.) And Pepper Arden facetiously rejected Wilberforce's warning of hell: "I hope things are not quite as bad as you say. I think a little whipping will do for me, not with any severity, I assure you." When Arden got older he admitted that his eternal destiny was no laughing matter. But it was too late; he died unregenerate. Wilberforce wept for his soul.[108] The death of Pitt, who never entered the fold of the faithful, was most grievous of all. "I own that I have a thousand times," Wilberforce wrote Muncaster, "wished and hoped that a quiet interval would be afforded him, perhaps in the evening of life, in which he and I might confer freely on the most important of all subjects. But the scene is closed—forever."[109]

Wilberforce's testimony as a Christian apologist preceded him, and his presence alone was occasionally enough to bring spiritual conviction. He often told the story of his "old friend, Lord N_____," whom he visited when sick. They sat for some time talking without Wilberforce making any reference to God or religion. When another friend walked in and asked the patient how he was doing, he replied: "As well as I can be, with Wilberforce sitting here and telling me I am going to hell."[110]

Though Wilberforce and his friends found this story amusing, there was nothing funny about the reality of hell; which is why, in addition to his many other human-itarian labors, he invested so much time, effort, and prayer into reaching his colleagues for Christ.

# Missions

*It has often been truly remarked . . . that the
moral character of a people may commonly be
known from the nature and attributes of the
objects of its worship.*[111]

ILBERFORCE'S PASSION FOR SOULS extended
beyond his immediate circle of friends and colleagues, and even beyond his beloved England. His sensitive imagination, contemplating the eternal destiny
of millions of heathens, abounded with compassion for
their souls. It is not surprising, then, that Wilberforce
was an early pioneer in the foreign missionary movement, especially in India.

As early as 1784, the year that Wilberforce's conversion began, it was acknowledged in the Commons
that Anglo-Indian relations were a "dire scandal and
confusion."[112] It was North's infamous East India Bill,
be it remembered, that sent Wilberforce and Pitt rush-

ing back to London from the French Court. The East India Company had been established in 1600 by royal charter as a trading company, intended to take advantage of the decline in Portugal's commercial power in the Far East. In the eighteenth century, rivalry between England and France broke out, but English supremacy was gained by the victories of Clive in the Seven Years' War (1756–63). From then on, England and the East India Company dominated the continent of India and profited from the warring native factions.

Throughout the company's long history in India, the British prided themselves on "honoring" the Indian civilization, which meant they viewed their relation as solely commercial without any moral or religious obligations. It was their public boast that "they never propagated their own religion," despite the obvious abominations of infanticide, suttee, and human sacrifice.[113]

Wilberforce, however, was of another mind. Having been strongly influenced by Charles Grant and John Shore, each of whom had lived for years in India under the employ of the East India Company, Wilberforce believed that England's commercial relationship with India brought with it corresponding moral and spiritual duties. Therefore, in 1793, when the company's charter was to be renewed, Wilberforce presented to Commons two resolutions, which had been drafted by Grant, requiring that the Company appoint chaplains both in India and aboard their merchantmen, and that the directors should send out suitable people to act as schoolmasters and missionaries. The resolutions passed the first two readings but were excluded from the final bill. Wilberforce lamented that "twenty millions of people are left to the providential protection of—Brahma."[114]

Despite the defeat, Wilberforce and the Saints continued their missionary efforts, since "it was not in their nature to accept defeat when they knew themselves to be in the right."[115] Sierra Leone, recently established in Africa, was now governed by Zachary Macaulay, and it freely admitted Methodist and Presbyterian missionaries who evangelized the surrounding territories. Australia also had earlier come to Wilberforce's attention when it had been chosen, in 1786, as a dumping ground for British convicts. In cooperation with Henry Thornton, he persuaded Pitt to appoint a chaplain (the Reverend Richard Johnson) to be settled with the prisoners in Botany Bay. Thus began a Christian witness in Australia in 1787. Wilberforce also took an active role in the formation of the Society for Missions to Africa and the East in 1799, which later became the Church Missionary Society; and he was instrumental in founding the British and Foreign Bible Society in 1803–4.

Meanwhile, India was not forgotten. Even though they lost the charter fight in 1793, the Saints did secure the appointment of Shore as the governor-general of India. And while he was not able to do much for their missionary schemes, he did build some new churches and provide shelter for William Carey and John Thomas, two Baptist missionaries who had arrived in India only months earlier. In 1794, Grant became the director of the East India Company and gained an appointment for a chaplain, Henry Martyn, to the company in 1805.

With the East India Company's charter up for renewal in 1813, Wilberforce, Grant, Shore, Simeon, Venn, and others maneuvered for victory. "We are all at work," he wrote in 1812, "about the best mode of providing for the free course of religious instruction in India."[116] In April, there was a general meeting of the Missionary Society, at which the members pledged themselves to promote Christianity in India. Clergymen were recruited, parliamentarians were lobbied, and the public was petitioned.

In February 1813, Wilberforce brought the question before Commons, presenting a petition of the Society for Promoting Christian Knowledge, requesting that the new charter make it legal to impart the teaching of Christianity in India. The initial response was not friendly. As the lobbying and letter writing continued, the decisive debate was set for June 22, 1813, in which Wilberforce gave one of his finest speeches. Pleading for the suffering multitudes of India he said:

> That remedy, Sir, is Christianity, . . . for Christianity assumes her true character, no less that she performs her natural and proper office, when she takes under her protection those poor degraded beings, on whom philosophy looks down with disdain, or perhaps with contemptuous condescension. On the very first promulgation of Christianity, it was declared by its great Author, as "glad tidings to the poor"; and, ever faithful to her character, Christian-

*ity still delights to instruct the ignorant, to succour the needy, to comfort the sorrowful, to visit the forsaken. . . .*

*Animated, Sir, by this unfeigned spirit of friendship of the natives of India, their religious and moral interests are undoubtedly our first concern; but the course we are recommending tends no less to promote their temporal well-being, than their eternal welfare; for such is their real condition, that we are prompted to endeavour to communicate to them the benefits of Christian instruction, scarcely less by religious principles than by the feelings of common humanity. Not, Sir, that I would pretend to conceal from the House, that the hope which, above all others, chiefly gladdens my heart, is that of being instrumental in bringing them into the paths by which they may be led to everlasting felicity.*[117]

Wilberforce then went on to describe the moral degradation of Indian society. There was, he said, the prevalent evil of infanticide, "against which we might have hoped that nature herself would have supplied adequate restraints, if we had not been taught by experience that for our deliverance even from this detestable crime we are indebted to Christianity." This was the "incorrigible vice of all antiquity" that Christianity had conquered in the West, but which was still practiced "where the light of Revelation has never penetrated. . . ."[118]

And then there was the detestable custom of suttee—the burning alive of widows on the funeral pyres of their husbands. These "horrible exhibitions" were so common that in Calcutta alone 130 widows were burned alive in the space of six months. Likewise hideous were "the various obscene and bloody rites of their idolatrous ceremonies, with all their unutterable abominations." Thousands were annually sacrificed in the service of their idols. The objects of their worship accounted for their horrendous moral condition: "Their divinities are absolute monsters of lust, injustice, wickedness, and cruelty. In short, their religious system is one grand abomination."[119]

Wilberforce concluded his speech with an appeal for immediate action, "to commence, with prudence, but with zeal, our endeavours to communicate to those benighted regions, the genial life and warmth of our Christian principles and institutions. . . ." It would be impossible for India not to find "Christianity the most powerful of all expedients for improving its morals, and promoting alike its temporal and eternal welfare."[120]

The three-hour speech struck home. Even one of his critics had to admit that "it was impossible not to be delighted with his eloquence. . . ."[121] In conjunction with more than eight hundred petitions that flooded into Commons, the House submitted to the oratory of Wilberforce and the Christian will of the English people. Both an Episcopal establishment and the first grant for Indian education were secured. And, of more importance, a door had been opened in India through which Christians from all the world could enter.

# Duty

*It is this which constitutes the character of
a real Christian: that, considering himself as
bought with a price—viz., that of the blood of
Jesus Christ—he regards it as his duty to try and
please his Saviour in everything.*[122]

*A*T A MINIMUM, DUTY MEANS honoring one's obligations. And for Wilberforce this meant honoring
his obligations to God above his obligations to others.
He felt duty bound to obey the claims of conscience, as
enlightened by the Scriptures, regardless of any unpleasant outcome.

It goes without saying that Wilberforce's life in politics was, in itself, a response to his sense of duty. After his
conversion he thought of leaving public life. He was now
shocked at the party spirit and self-aggrandizement that
prevailed in Commons. His political calling also entailed

a social life that was a constant source of temptation and trial to him. Yet duty required he "mix in the assemblies of men." And so he did.

On a number of occasions Wilberforce's public station meant he had to choose between his sense of duty and his personal feelings. As a general rule he believed it was his duty to support the government (which often meant supporting Pitt). Thus, when war broke out with France he felt obliged to support the war effort in order to honor treaties, even though he had a great disgust for bloodshed. In December of 1792 he addressed the House:

> *He [Wilberforce] frankly declared that, as at all time war ought to be deprecated as the greatest of human evils, so there never was a period when it appeared more likely to be injurious to this country than the present. . . . If we should find ourselves compelled by the obligations of solemn treaties to engage in war, as men of conscience and integrity we must submit to the necessity; but nothing less than this necessity would justify the [war] measure.*

Wilberforce detested the French Revolution and the French lust for blood, but he detested war even more. Yet, once war was declared, it was his duty to support the government. "I deemed it the part of a good subject not to use language which might tend to prevent the unanimity which was so desirable at the outset of such a war."[123]

As the war became protracted and took its toll on the country he believed that peace ought to be pursued.

Writing to Lord Muncaster he said: "I begin to think we can look for no good from the prosecution of the war; and if so, it is time to stop for a while the ravages of that scourge of the human species."[124] Accordingly, he was put in the difficult situation of opposing his dear friend Pitt. But what was more important, friendship or duty? Writing to Edward Eliot he struggled with the painful outcome of choosing the path of duty: "I need hardly say that the prospect of a public difference with Pitt is extremely painful to me, and, though I trust his friendship for me has sunk too deep in his heart to be soon worn out, I confess it hangs on me like a weight I cannot remove when I anticipate the whole situation. My spirits are hardly equal to the encounter. However I hope it will please God to enable me to act the part of an honest man on this trying occasion."[125]

Wilberforce chose duty. In December of 1794 he moved an amendment calling for peace. This was, in effect, open opposition to Pitt, and it shook them both. It has been said that only two public events ever caused Pitt to lose sleep. One was the mutiny at the Nore, the other was Wilberforce's open opposition to him during the war. Wilberforce also took it hard but felt compelled to act in response to his sense of duty. Writing later he said: "No one who has not seen a good deal of public life and felt how painful and difficult it is to differ widely from those with whom you wish to agree, can judge at what an expense of feeling such duties are performed."[126] The result was a serious, if brief, breach in their friendship.

On another occasion, the impeachment of Dundas, Wilberforce again had to publicly oppose his longtime friend. In February 1805, a Committee of Navy Inquiry presented a report that included accusations against Dundas, now Lord Melville. Melville was really the most indispensable member of Pitt's government. He had rebuilt the navy, he managed the House, and he maintained Scottish loyalty to Pitt. He was Pitt's closest political adviser.

The case against Melville was that he had permitted the misappropriation of funds by his subordinates. The evidence against his subordinates was compelling, and so a resolution of censure was moved in April. As the House debated the resolution, it became clear to Wilberforce that he must speak against Melville, and hence against Pitt. Moreover, on moral issues such as this, his voice was often decisive. His silence might save Melville, but he could not, for duty's sake, be silent. As he rose to speak he caught Pitt's pleading eye: "It required no little effort to resist the fascination of that penetrating eye."[127] Yet resist he did. He told the House, "I really cannot find language sufficiently strong to express my utter detestation of such conduct."[128] The speech swayed Commons and the resolution passed. Pitt was overcome. The prime minister who had endured disasters, wars, and rebellion—the man who was known as a paragon of self-composure—lost himself. He broke down in tears and was ushered out of the House by his supporters.

There is no doubt that Wilberforce had, both then and throughout his life, a profound love and admiration for Pitt. Yet the claims of duty are stronger than the cords of friendship. This is a bitter truth, yet true nonetheless. A leader who would fulfill the claims of his conscience must at times forgo the comforts of his comrades. A leader will do his duty even if it means standing alone.

# PRINCIPLE

*Policy, however, Sir, is not my principle, and I
am not ashamed to say it. There is a principle
above everything that is politic, and when I
reflect on the command which says: "Thou shalt
do no murder," believing its authority to be
divine, how can I dare to set up any reasonings
of my own against it?*[129]

$S$INCE WILBERFORCE SPENT NEARLY forty-five years in
Parliament, it may be surprising to learn that he had
a strong dislike for politics. Not that he thought civil government was, in itself, evil. The problem was not government; rather, it was the type of men who governed and
how the machinery of government was run.

When he arrived in London as a "freshman" M.P.,
he really expected to find an elevated moral and intellectual tone. We know, of course, that he found just the

opposite. Yes, there were many bright lights in Parliament, yet there was a moral insouciance that, after his conversion, he found distasteful if not disgusting. For many members in Parliament, government was simply a mode to fulfill one's personal ambitions for fame, power, or wealth. It was not, as Wilberforce thought it should be, a principled enterprise. Writing to a friend in 1802 he mentioned his impatience at "so much sang-froid in this benevolent age," and that he was quite sickened by public men.[130] Any taint of corruption in high places was inexcusable, which explains his vote against Melville.

Because he was one of those unique phenomena in the political world—a principled politician—Wilberforce remained independent and would not join a party. A "party spirit" was to him a source of political corruption. A man should be free to vote according to principle; better, he should be loyal to principle over party. He loathed "party" as a source of political dissension, which was a disease in the body politic. In a memorandum found after his death, Wilberforce denounces "party principles." It is "our duty," he writes,

> *to condemn the first open avowal of these shameless principles, to denounce them as public enemies, to raise the hue and cry, as it were, of the country against them as common enemies to the peace and order of civil society . . . they are in reality base in their extraction, mean and low and sordid in their nature, as they are mischievous in their tendency and operation. . . . The effects of party are pernicious beyond all measure, sapping*

> *the foundations of our greatness and glory, of our strength, our energies, our eternal happiness and comfort. . . . It is achieving the ruin of our country. I hate it, just in proportion as I love my country.*[131]

Because Wilberforce usually voted in Pitt's favor, the opposition sneered at his "independence." However, Wilberforce happened to agree with Pitt in most cases. And when he did not, he would vote against him, as we have seen. Moreover, he felt that Pitt had to a degree been corrupted by the practice of using "influence" in government rather than standing firmly on principle.

In his own case, Wilberforce would never use his influence with Pitt, or his power in Commons, to gain any advantages or favors for himself or others. In a letter to Pitt in January 1805, he asserted that, as a matter of principle, he never abused their friendship by asking for favors for constituents. The truth of his assertion is borne out by his response to the insistent requests of his friend Clarkson to use his influence to gain for his brother a captaincy in the navy. After being rebuked by Clarkson for not pressing the matter with Lord Chatham, Wilberforce told his demanding friend it was a matter of principle not "to truck and barter away any personal influence I may possess with some of the members of the Administration, which ought to be preserved entire for opportunities of public service."[132]

Whenever he lobbied for the appointment of a clergyman, for instance, he always tried to have "serious" Evangelicals selected, even if their appointment did not solidify his political alliances. Once, when a supporter

wrote asking for a "living" for a clerical friend, Wilberforce replied with uncharacteristic harshness:

> *I am sorry to be now under the Necessity of inform-*
> *ing you that I am so circumstanced at present as*
> *not to have it in my Power to comply with your*
> *Request without Impropriety. I feel it however my*
> *Duty not to conclude without frankly avowing to*
> *you the Circumstance of yourself and your Friend*
> *having some Interest in Yorkshire would in no*
> *degree influence me in your Favour on the present*
> *Occasion, and I confess that I wonder you should*
> *suggest this consideration in such a connection.*
> *Upon reflection you cannot I think but disapprove*
> *of it as a Sentiment equally dishonourable to me to*
> *whom it is suggested, and to yourself from whom*
> *it comes. Having said this with a Freedom I think*
> *it right to use, I will add that I am conscious there*
> *are many Persons who conceive themselves as*
> *at liberty to employ for the advancement of their*
> *Political Interest, any Influence they may possess in*
> *the disposal of ecclesiastical preferments, and you*
> *may without much thought have then given in to a*
> *Practice, which from what you tell me of your Con-*
> *nections you cannot I think but condemn on more*
> *mature deliberations.*[133]

In light of such plain speaking, it is striking to learn
that Wilberforce had a reputation for equivocation.
Members listened to his speeches with anticipation but
often were unsure how he would vote. Once, after a

speech, Whitbread jumped up and said: "Mr. Speaker, my Honourable Friend who has just sat down has as usual spoken on *both sides of the Question.*" The House roared with laughter. A friend of Sidmouth's met Wilberforce and said that he was "a great courtier without any fixed opinion, except on the Slave Trade and the essential doctrines of Christianity."[134] In reality, Wilberforce had very fixed opinions on many issues; however, he was willing to consider all sides of a question and was very charitable to believe the best of his opponents. As he said, "we should examine circumspectly on all sides, and abide by that opinion which, on carefully balancing all considerations, appears fairly entitled to our preference."[135] His temporizing was not duplicity. On the contrary, he vacillated because he was scrupulously honest and sought to make all his decisions according to principles of truth and justice.

George Stephen, the youngest son of James, spent his childhood around Wilberforce and knew him well. Years later, in his *Anti-Slavery Recollections*, he summed up Wilberforce's principled approach to political questions:

> *Men might doubt about his vote on minor issues, but where the interest of morality, or humanity, or religion were involved, there Wilberforce's perception of what was right appeared intuitive, and his vote was certain: neither rank, nor power, nor eloquence bewildered him for a moment. All the honours, all the wealth, all the seductions that the world could furnish, would not have tempted him to offend his conscience by even a momentary*

> *hesitation; he at once rose above all infirmities of habit, firm as a rock upon the spiritual foundation on which he rested.*[136]

# CRITICISM

*A person in a public station must often
acquiesce under the grossest calumnies, unless
he will undertake the vain and endless task of
contradicting all the falsehoods which prejudice
may conceive, and malignity propagate
against him.*[137]

WILBERFORCE'S PRINCIPLED POLITICS won him both
acclaim and criticism, fame and infamy. Those
who disagreed with his causes and religion were often
bitterly slanderous toward him. They could hardly tolerate a man who dared to mix religion and politics, morality and legislation. The more things change, the more
they stay the same. Calumny is the reward for character.
A principled leader must brace himself for war.

The slave interests, in particular, were singularly hostile toward Wilberforce and his colleagues. Of course, people who would brutalize and enslave innocent people—beating them like animals, or casting them to sharks like bait—are not scrupulous to use lesser forms of murder such as "the poisoned arrows of calumny and falsehood."[138] For example, their malicious temper was displayed in their glee over the death of abolitionist James Ramsay. In the early years of the debate, the West Indian Planters spread vile rumors about Ramsay, claiming that his former days were "one black story of depravity." Though the rumors were false, and were even refuted by an investigation by James Stephen, Ramsay's sensitive nature gave way to the poison, and he died from the strain and abuse. Mr. Molyneux, a West Indian planter, proudly announced to his son, "Ramsay is dead—and I have killed him."[139]

The slave traders were no less kind to Wilberforce himself. Early in the campaign a Mr. Morris, who had lost his temper under Wilberforce's cross-examination, threatened his life. Somewhat later another captain named Rolleston challenged Wilberforce to a duel, which he evaded on principle. And then there was the case of a Mr. Kimber, whom Wilberforce had exposed in Commons because he had murdered a Negro girl. The charge was true but Kimber was acquitted, said Wilberforce, "through the shameful remissness of the Crown Lawyers." Kimber harassed Wilberforce and demanded not only a public apology but also five thousand pounds in cash and a place in the government. Upon his refusal, Kimber accosted Wilberforce in public and even came to his home uttering threats, which were taken seriously: Lord Rokeby offered Wilberforce to ride in his coach while he himself carried a loaded pistol. Fortunately, Kimber was placated by the intervention of Lord Sheffield.[140]

The slave interests also spread vile rumors and ridiculous gossip about Wilberforce. Once, when Clarkson was doing his investigations, a fellow passenger told him, "Mr. Wilberforce is no doubt a great philanthropist in public; but I happen to know a little of his private history, and can assure you that he is a cruel husband and beats his wife." Wilberforce, it so happened, was still a bachelor. That, however, did not deter his detractors; it only added to the scandal. For they rumored he was not only secretly married, but that his wife was a Negro woman.[141]

Of course, any disturbances or slave uprisings were immediately imputed to Wilberforce and the abolitionists. When the slaves revolted in Barbados, damaging sixty estates but killing no Europeans, Wilberforce was again singled out for abuse. "Mr. Wilberforce and his adherents . . . have created a volcano," wrote Langford Hodge.[142] The planters' invectives were more violent than ever before. Yet Wilberforce wrote to Stephen, "A more scandalous attack I have seldom seen, but I am rather animated than discouraged by it. . . . I get more and more to disrelish these brawlings and to be less and less touchy as to my character."[143]

Moreover, Wilberforce and his allies were accused of being closet revolutionaries. After war with France broke, Lord Abingdon said, "All abolitionists are Jacobins."

And George III told Lord Portland, "I always told Mr. Pitt they were hypocrites and not to be trusted." The royal family as a whole was against Wilberforce. The Prince of Wales declared that Wilberforce was "Republican at heart," while the duke of Clarence pronounced in the Lords that "the promoters of the Abolition were either frauds or hypocrites, and in one of those classes" was Wilberforce.[144]

Boswell, who had initially recruited Wilberforce for the cause, later became a turncoat and lambasted him in public doggerel:

> *Go, W—, with narrow skull,*
> *Go home and preach away at Hull.*
> *No longer to the senate cackle*
> *In strains that suit the tabernacle,*
> *I hate your little wittling sneer,*
> *Your pert and self-sufficient leer,*
> *Mischief to trade sits on your lips,*
> *Insects will gnaw the noblest ships.*
> *Go, W—, begone, for shame,*
> *Thou dwarf with big resounding name.*[145]

The irony, not to mention the inaccuracy, of calling Wilberforce a Jacobin is evident from the fact that the Jacobins themselves bitterly detested him. Because he devoted the majority of his time and energy to the cause of abolition rather than working-class problems, and because he supported the government's repressive wartime measures, he was vilified by the true Jacobins. William Hazlit, in his book *The Spirit of the Age*, charged that Wilberforce "acts from mixed motives. He would willingly serve God and Mammon." After the Peterloo incident, Francis Place called him "an ugly epitome of the devil."[146]

But perhaps his most violent critic was the radical Cobbett. After Wilberforce published his *Appeal* in 1823, Cobbett published a response in which he called Wilberforce's book "a great deal of canting trash; a great deal of lying; a great deal of that cool impudent falsehood for which the Quakers are famed. . . . There is no man who knows anything at all of the real situation of the Blacks, who will not declare you to be totally ignorant of the subject on which you are writing, or to be a most consummate hypocrite." Cobbett claimed that the slaves were living a life of ease compared to the oppressed British laborers. "You seem to have a great affection for the fat and lazy and laughing and singing and dancing negroes," he chided. The most absurd charge of all—one that Cobbett knew to be false—followed: "Never have you done one single act in favour of the labourers of this country."[147]

The answer to these obloquies is obvious, as historian Carpenter has succinctly stated: "The colossal labours of his whole life speak for themselves."[148]

As every leader must learn, criticism is the tribute that vice pays to virtue. And in the final analysis, there is no better refutation of slander than a life well lived. Virtue, like wisdom, is justified by her children.

# ADVERSITY

*We ought not to expect this life to flow on
smoothly without rubs or mortifications.*[149]

ANYONE NOT FAMILIAR WITH THE FACTS of Wilberforce's life might be tempted to think he lived
a life of undisturbed ease. He was, after all, wealthy,
popular, and powerful. He rubbed shoulders with society's elite. He was on personal terms with royalty. He
could afford the best food, the best wine, the best books,
the best horses, the best equipage any English gentleman
could want. He seemed to live in that mythical mount
of the gods where carnal feasting and courtly pleasure
shielded him from mortal woes.

If only it were so.

The fact was, Wilberforce, like the rest of us, experienced his share of earthly sorrows. The rarefied air of

upper-class living was no aegis from the adversity that is the lot of every man—even of every leader. Advantage was tempered by affliction.

One of his greatest difficulties was a lifelong battle against poor health. He was so frail at birth that he would have been abandoned, he said, had he been born in pagan times. He barely escaped the fate of his two sisters who died before reaching majority. His eyes were always bad, an ailment he inherited from his mother, and he eventually lost the sight in one of them. Thus his handwriting was black and bold until old age when he used a magnifying glass for writing in his diary. Throughout his career he wore an eyeglass on a riband. Due to years of opium use he often started the day in near blindness.

In January of 1788 Wilberforce fell ill, the first of many such physical lapses. He had fallen sick on January 10, but continued to work until February 19, when exhaustion, fever, and loss of appetite overcame him. On the twenty-third he saw Dr. Pitcairne, the renowned Scottish physician, who was unable to help. Wilberforce struggled to continue his work: "I am still a close prisoner, wholly unequal even to such little business as I am now engaged in: add to which my eyes are so bad that I can scarce see how to direct my pen." He was ordered to Bath to recuperate, but before he could leave he completely broke down with fever, recurrent diarrhea, debility and no appetite—all symptoms of ulcerative colitis. Fearing the worst, Lord Muncaster sent for his mother and sister, and called Dr. Warren, famous for his treatment of the king. The verdict was grim: "He had not the stamina to last a fortnight."[150] Both Warren and Pitcairne agreed that opium was his only hope. Accordingly he was placed on the drug and sent to Bath. By the end of the year he was well enough to return to Commons.

Lapses such as these were a constant vexation. In March of 1796, after the disappointing abolition defeat of 70–74, Wilberforce again fell ill. Milner rushed from Cambridge and nursed him back to health. "He was the means," said Wilberforce, "if not of saving my life, at least of sparing me a long and dangerous fit of sickness. . . ."[151] Only a few years later, in 1799, his health was so poor that his doctors urged him to retire from Commons for at least a year. He then went to Bath with Barbara, and when John Venn saw his deteriorated condition he urged him not to return to London: "You are not in state to bear the hurry and fatigue of a winter residence in Town. . . . Your constitution is not robust and you must not endeavour to do what would break down even the stoutest constitution."[152] Wilberforce ignored his advice. In 1801 he was again sick. By 1807 he was having trouble with his lungs, and two years later he developed curvature of the spine. One of his shoulders began to slope and his neck began to fall forward. Thus, when only fifty years old he had to wear a steel girdle, or brace, covered with leather for comfort. From then on, Wilberforce repeatedly fought against the potent forces of deathly decay.

Death, of course, struck his consciousness at an early age. When he was only nine years old he lost his father, a blow softened only by the kind attention of his uncle. As an adult he suffered many bereavements. He buried his mother, as well as many of his dearest friends. Edward Eliot died in 1797 and William Pitt in 1806. Granville

Sharp passed away in July of 1813, and by September of the same year, Muncaster was dead. Other fellow warriors followed their descent.

But worst of all, Wilberforce lost his two daughters. By the autumn of 1821 his elder daughter, Barbara, began a serious decline from "consumption." She was taken to Bath but returned to London in December for medical advice. By Christmas Day she was nearly gone. Wilberforce looked to God as, with a broken heart, he watched her fade away. On December 30 she was pronounced dead. Only the consolations of God's Word and the "assured persuasion of Barbara's happiness" in heaven took away "the sting of death."[153] Little over ten years later, in February 1832, his remaining daughter, Lizzy, fell ill with a pulmonary complaint. And before she could be moved to St. Boniface, she died. Wilberforce took it hard, and a friend thought it aged him noticeably. Surely there is no use of the pen more bitter than writing your child's epitaph.

One would think that, after a long life of service to his nation and to mankind, God would have allowed Wilberforce to spend his final years in repose. But as it turned out, he was again struck by criticism and adversity. When he moved to Highwood he found that the parish church was too far away from many of the cottagers, so he planned to build a chapel nearby. He approached the vicar of Hendon, a Mr. Williams, who initially supported the idea. However, as the edifice began to rise, so did Williams's jealousy. He then turned on Wilberforce, accusing him in a pamphlet of "prosecuting by the grossest falsehood a scheme for my own and my family's pecuniary gain under the pretended motive of promoting the spiritual interests of my poor neighbors."[154] Moreover, his son William, as mentioned earlier, ruined his father's fortune through improvident business dealings, leaving Wilberforce without a final home.

Wilberforce's adversity would have crushed a man of lesser faith and fortitude. Yet he overcame his handicaps by the vitality of his curiosity and the urgency of his calling. Through it all, whether public criticism or private hardship, he leaned on the arm of Almighty God. This little fellow with the calico guts, who was not to last a fortnight, outlived his enemies and overcame his adversities. He conquered through faith in God and submission to his will.

# SELF-CONTROL

*Some self-indulgence perhaps may have lost us
an advantage, the benefit of which might have
extended through life.*[155]

*W*ILBERFORCE REALIZED THAT IN ORDER to fulfill his
calling as a world-changing leader, he must willingly sacrifice innocent pleasures. Indeed, when it comes
to leadership, the difference between greatness and medi-
ocrity is commonly the difference between discipline and
indulgence. Before he can govern others, a leader must
first govern himself.

Shortly after his conversion, Wilberforce became
convinced that many "common gratifications" were unac-
ceptable for him as a Christian and a public leader. The
following memorandum on "the temptations of the table"
shows his determination to master his appetites:

> *After dining with Pitt, tête-à-tête I find after a time*
> *I have been giving way to the temptations of the*
> *table against the sharpest convictions of the crimi-*
> *nality of the compliances, for little as they might*
> *seem what sins are they disqualify me from every*
> *useful purpose.*
>
> *I see Bob Smith who is influenced by inferior*
> *considerations, I see Pitt too and others of my*
> *friends practising self denial and restraint in these*
> *respects, and when they exceed tis at times of jol-*
> *lity, whereas I do it merely from the Brutal Sensual-*
> *ity of animal Gratification. I trust I shall better keep*
> *than I have done the resolutions of temperance that*
> *I make at this moment.*
>
> *Simplicity. In Quantity moderate—as little*
> *thought About my eating and drinking as possible*
> *either before or after—Never more than six glasses*
> *of wine, my common allowance two or three . . .*
> *to be in bed always if possible by eleven and be up*
> *by six o'clock. The effect on my Health should be*
> *attended to; a full diet good for me, but a simple*
> *one, no sweet, no rich things, no mixtures.*[156]

As Wilberforce was recovering from the first onslaught of colitis, he determined, for both physical and spiritual reasons, to be self-controlled in bodily pleasures. This was a great challenge, of course, since dining and drinking were part of his station as a politician. When he went to Rayrigg (a house he rented on Lake Windermere) in the summer of 1788, he was hounded by the duchess of Gordon, who was a leading Tory hostess. She came "tapping at our low window" and "would take no denial." After many entreaties, she persuaded Wilberforce and Milner to take supper with her, an experience that confirmed Wilberforce's need for self-control. Not many days later he wrote in his diary:

> *The life I am now leading is unfavourable in all*
> *respects, both to mind and body, as little suited to*
> *me as an invalid . . . as it is becoming my character*
> *and profession as a Christian. Indolence and intem-*
> *perance are its capital features. It is true, the inces-*
> *sant intrusion of fresh visitors, and the constant*
> *temptations to which I am liable, from always being*
> *in company, render it extremely difficult to adhere*
> *to any plan of study, or any resolutions of abstemi-*
> *ousness, which last too it is the harder for me to*
> *observe, because my health requires throughout an*
> *indulgent regime. Nothing can excuse or palliate*
> *such conduct. . . .*[157]

Wilberforce's fastidiousness would have struck his contemporaries (had it been known) as a sign of "enthusiasm," whereas it might strike many moderns as a symptom of neurosis. On the contrary, he believed that gluttony was "the lowest and most debasing of all gratifications," and that overindulgence in either food or drink was a form of "intemperance" that made him unfit for "every useful purpose in life."[158]

Perhaps the most striking example of Wilberforce's self-control was his moderate and disciplined use of opium, that most potent and seductive of remedies. Opium was a favorite eighteenth-century medicine, prescribed for a variety of ailments: migraines, vertigo, intestinal problems, insomnia, and others. It was openly bought at chemists' or druggists' just as were other medicines. There was no restriction on its sale, and it was even used in a soothing syrup for infants and a popular tonic for children, "Godfrey's Cordial." Dean Milner used opium for digestive problems, and the poet George Crabbe had it prescribed (and used it the remainder of his life) after he collapsed in the street from dizziness. Even Hannah More used it temporarily for a nervous condition. Some doctors disputed its value and potential harm, but there was no stigma attached to its use, as can be seen from Wilberforce's critics never raising the issue. As a medicinal remedy, opium presented no moral dilemma.

On the other hand, there were concerns about potential side effects and dependency, which probably explains Wilberforce's initial hesitation to commence its use. Nevertheless, opium saved his life; and thereafter, it was necessary for him to take it daily. From 1788 to his death in 1833, he maintained a consistently low dose of five grains daily, or one pill, three times a day (after breakfast, after tea, and at bedtime).[159] Though occasionally, due to severe illness, he had to increase the amount, he always lowered his dosage to the previous level.

It would be wrong to call Wilberforce an "addict," as that term is used today. Addiction is a sign of mental or emotional weakness and leads to the deterioration of a person's life. Dependency, in contrast, is a medical necessity and leads to the improvement of one's life. Wilberforce was clearly dependent, just as a diabetic is dependent on insulin. Instead of his opium dependency being a sign of weakness, his ability to control its use and resist its hidden charms was a sign of great moral strength. The biographer Pollock is right to say, "It is proof of the strength of his will that he achieved so much under a burden which neither he nor his doctors understood."[160]

Not only did Wilberforce learn to master the appetites common to all, he had to master the additional temptations of an elixir that had enslaved such notables as De Quincey and Coleridge.[161] Due to the strength of his moral character and self-control, however, he became the master of all. The man who freed the slaves was first a freeman himself.

# MARRIAGE

*It is a favorite opinion of mine . . . that to
the institution of marriage, as it exists in all
countries where Christianity prevails, is to be
ascribed that superiority which is so marked
in the European over Asiatic natives. . . . At
first sight we observe something to admire and
love, but the more closely we inspect, the more
thoroughly we examine, so much the more cause
do we find for love and admiration.*[162]

IOGRAPHERS HAVE NOT BEEN KIND to Wilberforce's
wife, Barbara. This is due, no doubt, to the contemporary sketch painted by the younger Marianne
Thornton, who grew up at Wilberforce's feet:

*She fell in love very suddenly, being the only reli-
gious member of a worldly family, and she confided
to Mr. Wilberforce all her persecutions and difficulties. She was extremely handsome and in some*

> *ways very clever, but very deficient in common*
> *sense, a woman with narrow views and selfish*
> *aims, that is, if selfishness can be so called when*
> *it took the shape of idolatry of her husband, and*
> *thinking everything in the world ought to give way*
> *to what she thought expedient for him.*
>
> *Instead of helping him forward in the great*
> *works which it appeared Providence had given him*
> *to do, she always considered she was hardly used*
> *when he left her side, and instead of making his*
> *home attractive to the crowds of superior people*
> *that he invited, her love of economy made her any-*
> *thing but an hospitable hostess. Yet the oddity and*
> *queerness of the scenes that went on there often*
> *made up, especially to young people, for all their*
> *deficiencies.*[163]

Marianne's mother (also named Marianne) was no kinder when she said, "No one would have known how much of an angel there was in Wilberforce if they had not seen his behaviour to one [Barbara] whose different tastes must have tried his patience so much."[164]

There is no question that the Thornton ladies idolized Wilberforce and found his choice of a "common" woman below his dignity. Indeed, it is hard to imagine exactly who might have passed the test of their jealous and possessive eyes. Furneaux is right when he comments that Marianne "loathed and envied Barbara almost as much as she loved Wilberforce. . . ."[165]

Wilberforce's other friends were more objective. Even though they had urged caution during his hasty courtship, they all spoke highly of her. For instance, Hannah More wrote: "She is a pretty, pleasing pious young woman, and I hope will make him happy." Zachary Macaulay, not one who easily parted with compliments, said: "Her exterior indicates great sweetness of temper, considerable humility, and a mind rather highly embellished than strongly cultivated."[166]

Really, the last thing Wilberforce wanted, or needed, was a pavilion-hopping, hobnobbing socialite—a busybody duchess or a self-indulgent "lady." For him nobility had lost its novelty; and horses, hounds, and hospitality their attraction. Wilberforce preferred a woman who was first of all "serious" in the religious sense—not only a Christian, but a woman of deep and pure piety. He also desired a "simple" woman. He had quite tired of the extravagant excesses of high society, and was content with a plainer lifestyle. Barbara's faith and habits suited him on both accounts. She was truly pious and intensely domestic. She existed, first and foremost, for the sake of her family (this is what Marianne meant by "narrow"). She was a devoted wife who looked after the frail health of her husband, and she was a nurturing mother who won the hearts of her children. "Never was there a tenderer or more loving mother," Samuel wrote, "rarely one more sensible or more really able."[167]

Not that she was flawless. At times she could be fussy, and she had a propensity to worry for the safety of her family. She also was economical nearly to a fault (whereas Wilberforce was generous nearly to a fault). She was a "homebody" and at times begrudged her husband being absent from home on official business. Nor was she an accommodating hostess; but then, who could have fully fed the beasts of Noah's ark? Wilberforce gladly overlooked her blemishes, as she overlooked his. They genuinely loved each other, and must have suited each other well; for throughout their entire marriage they were blissfully happy together.

Henry Thornton's judgment of Barbara was more balanced, and accurate, than his daughter's:

> *She is a very pleasing young woman about twenty-five, rather handsome than otherwise, with character, and unquestionably of a pious disposition. Her fortune is small (5,000 pounds) and the family is not by any means grand, her father being merely a thriving merchant and a country banker with a large family. They live six miles from Birmingham—the name is Spooner. The match is not what the world would account to be a good match—that is to say he [Wilberforce] has not insisted on some things which the world most esteems, because he has thought it indispensable that the lady should have certain other qualities.*[168]

That last sentence is most telling. Those "certain other qualities" that Wilberforce wanted in a wife are described in his own words. "I believe her to be a real Christian," he wrote, "affectionate, sensible, rational in habits, moderate in desires and pursuits, capable of bearing prosperity without intoxication, and adversity without repining."[169]

Throughout thirty-five years of marriage Wilberforce never changed his early opinion of Barbara. A higher commendation by a husband could not be written.

# FAMILY

*It is of great importance to preserve boys'
affections, and prevent their thinking home a
dull place.*[170]

CONSIDERING THAT WILBERFORCE was a "confirmed
bachelor" when he finally married at the age
of thirty-seven, it is amazing how well this benedict
adjusted to family life. He was both a faithful husband
and an affectionate father who, despite his many pressing
public duties, did not neglect his family.

Wilberforce took fatherhood seriously. As his family
began to grow, he realized that he needed a better balance in his life between work and home. By 1807 he
was the father of two girls (Barbara and Elizabeth) and
four boys (William, Robert Isaac, Samuel, and Henry
William). When his youngest was five, Wilberforce relin-
quished his powerful seat as an M.P. for Yorkshire and

took the inferior post of Bramber so he could spend more time with his growing children. "As to my plan of life," he wrote, "I conceive that my chief object should be, first, my children; secondly, Parliament."[171]

Next to Barbara, his children were his chief delight. His home was often a scene of convivial confusion, with his older sons running around as "clever amusing restless little creatures, kept in very little order, though they had a large retinue of governesses and tutors, and friends who acted half as governesses and tutors."[172] While most upper-class men of Wilberforce's time tended to be distant from their children, he was an indulgent father who took his children on holidays, read them books, played cricket (even though William's fastball damaged his foot), and would plop down on the floor for games. As he terminated one letter, "I am irresistibly summoned to a game of marbles."[173]

The powerful politician was a playful papa. Charles Shore, a family friend, commented on how his young boys would take advantage of Wilberforce's playfulness:

> On a visit I observed him during a considerable time walking round the lawn followed by three of these striplings. Whilst he selected each in his turn as his companion, the other two amuse themselves with practical jokes of which he was the victim. Repeatedly brought to bay, and remonstrating with his persecutors, each of whom in turn profited by his instructive converse, he passed much of his time fruitlessly on the defensive.[174]

With the stress of his political duties, philanthropic projects, imploring guests, and nagging health, it is a wonder he was so at peace when thronged with six noisy children. They would hang around his desk or run through the house when he was working. Once, a friend was with Wilberforce in his library at Kensington Gore while he was looking for an important letter. Wilberforce began to look vexed. Just at that moment came thunderous noise from the nursery upstairs. "Now for once," his friend thought, "Wilberforce's temper will give way." But as he turned, an angelic smile was on his face. "What a blessing to have these dear children!" he sighed. "Only think what a relief, amidst other hurries, to hear their voices and know they are well."[175]

Wilberforce tended to his children's education by sending them to small private schools. Like most Evangelicals, he regarded the public schools as "hotbeds of vice." When his sons were older, William was sent to Trinity College, Cambridge. He was charming like his father but "without energy of character or solid principle of action."[176] He did poorly in school and withdrew. Later he plunged the family into debt; yet after much heartache, settled down. His other sons attended Oriel and distinguished themselves as scholars.

His children's spiritual welfare concerned Wilberforce the most. As he wrote, "the spiritual interests of my children is my first object."[177] He had family devotions twice a day, and he was continually admonishing his children to seek Christ and walk in his ways. It was his duty, he felt, to nurture their souls just as a gardener does his fruit trees. Writing to nine-year-old Samuel he said:

*I was shocked to hear that you are nine years old;*
*I thought it was eight. You must take great pains to*
*prove to me that you are nine not in years only, but*
*in head and heart and mind. Above all, my dear-*
*est Samuel, I am anxious to see decisive marks of*
*your having begun to undergo the great change. I*
*come again and again to look to see if it really be*
*begun, just as a gardener walks up again and again*
*to examine his fruit trees and see if his peaches are*
*set; if they are swelling and becoming larger, finally*
*if they are becoming ripe and rosy. I would willingly*
*walk barefoot from this place to Sandgate to see a*
*clear proof of the grand change being begun in my*
*dear Samuel at the end of my journey.*[178]

Again he writes to Samuel almost three years later:

*Loving you as dearly as I do, It might seem strange*
*to some thoughtless people that I am glad to hear*
*you are unhappy. But as it is about your soul, as I*
*know that a short unhappiness of this kind often*
*leads to lasting happiness and peace and joy, I*
*cannot but rejoice. I trust, my dear boy, it is the*
*Spirit of God knocking at the door of your heart,*
*as the Scripture expresses it, and making you feel*
*uneasy, that you may be driven to find pardon and*
*the sanctifying influences of the Holy Spirit, and*
*so be made one of Christ's flock and be taken care*
*of in this world and be delivered from hell, and be*
*taken when you die, whether sooner or later, to*
*everlasting happiness in heaven. My dearest boy,*

> *whenever you feel in this way, I beseech you, get*
> *alone and fall on your knees, and pray as earnestly as*
> *you can to God for Christ's sake to forgive you and*
> *to sanctify you, and in short to make you to be born*
> *again, as our Saviour expressed it to Nicodemus.*[179]

Exhortations of this kind permeate Wilberforce's letters to his children, and surely reflect the nature of his paternal instruction at home. Happily, the arrows of admonition hit the target: all of his children became true Christians (a great consolation when his two daughters died), and three of his sons took holy orders. Each was earnest in the exercise of his pastoral duties, with Samuel becoming a renowned Victorian clergyman and bishop.

Because a man's heart is indivisible, his private and public life are inseparable. Wilberforce's greatness as a leader was mirrored in his goodness at home. And it is the home that is the sure touchstone of all civic greatness. The fire of the hearth purifies the altar and purges the throne.

# VISION

*The Supreme Disposer of all things can turn
the hearts of men, and before Him difficulties
vanish.*[180]

THERE ARE THREE ELEMENTS to any sound definition of *vision*. The first is imagination, or the ability to "see" with the mind's eye what is not presented to the senses. Second, there must be that "hope which maketh not ashamed," or the belief that the vision is actually attainable. And third, there must be constructive action toward making the mental vision a concrete reality. Without these three elements a leader will be a mere visionary and not a man of vision.

It has often been asked how "enlightened" eighteenth-century England could not only tolerate but actually sanction slavery and the slave trade. It appears a mystery to many moderns that such an obvious and blatant evil could be casually winked at. One reason is that for most Englishmen slavery was not a "visible" evil. Relatively speaking, there were very few slaves in England, and those who lived there were usually domestic servants. The brutality of gang slavery on the plantations was never observed firsthand. And the same holds true for the infamous Middle Passage. Its horrors were out of sight and thus out of mind: "No squeamish folk in England ever saw the conditions under which the slaves were bought, transported and resold. All that was visible to them were the goods they had helped to make. . . ."[181]

It is a tribute to Wilberforce's vision that he had the ability to see the invisible. And it is remarkable that though he never peered into the bowels of a slave ship, nor stepped foot on a plantation, he was able to envision the suffering and terror of the poor slaves. Ramsay's reports and Clarkson's accounts stirred his sensitive imagination. The cracking whip, the painful shrieks, the bloody backs, the brutal deaths—these were realities to him. "His crusade," notes Warner, "was based on imaginative sympathy."[182] Thus, after the disappointing loss in 1805, Wilberforce wrote: "I could not sleep after waking the first night. The poor blacks rushed into my mind, and the guilts of our wicked land." Again, writing to Muncaster: "I could not sleep either on Thursday or Friday night, without dreaming of scenes of depredation and cruelty on the injured shore of Africa. . . ."[183] In 1818, after hearing of the murder of a slave, he wrote, "My mind becomes so affected by the sad state of these poor injured wretches that it keeps me awake at night."[184]

Wilberforce's vision also included hope. It is true that there was already a multitude of sundry voices condemning slavery: Locke,[185] Baxter,[186] Johnson,[187] the Quakers,[188] the Methodists.[189] But it is possible to protest without really believing things will ever change. It is more a lamentation, or declaration of despair, rather than a battle cry, which is a declaration of hope.

Wilberforce, however, actually had the audacity to believe that the detestable evil of slavery could be abolished. Because he trusted in the God of the Bible, he knew that God was on the side of the just, and that if he opposed human oppression he would be supported by the Almighty himself. That was the key to his perseverance, as he said: "Our motto must continue to be perseverance. And ultimately I trust that the Almighty will crown our efforts with success."[190]

Last, Wilberforce's vision inspired him to action. "He could not be a passive spectator of any undertaking," noted Stephen, "which had the welfare of mankind for its object."[191] Denunciation, declamation, protest—these, in and of themselves, were not enough. Denouncing evil without constructive action is no better than whining. That, he understood. Once the banner is raised, the army must charge. And that is exactly what Wilberforce did. Once he accepted the leadership of the abolition movement, he began to plan and act for change. He sent out Clarkson on his fact-finding expeditions, he enlisted Macaulay for legal research, he lobbied Pitt to move the Privy Council to investigate the trade, and he and Babington began their rigorous preparation for debate. And this was only the beginning. For nearly twenty years Wilberforce continued to study, write, organize, petition, lobby, and do everything in his power to see his vision become a reality.

In his last speech in the Commons, in June of 1824, Wilberforce exhorted the House not to tamper with the feelings of the slaves who were hoping for freedom; for, he said, "hope deferred maketh the heart sick." True it is. And it is a monument to the strength of Wilberforce's vision that he never, in the long and arduous struggle against slavery, abandoned hope.

# REFORM

*But there is an established order in God's
government, or sure connexion between vice
and misery, which through the operation of
natural causes, works out His will and vindicates
His moral government.*[192]

WILBERFORCE'S VISIONARY LEADERSHIP and moral
conviction inevitably thrust him into the role
of a reformer. He was one of the key players in the abolition of two of the most horrendous evils of his day, the
slave trade and slavery. In addition, his vision extended
to a host of other causes that were ahead of their time.
He labored for moral, legal, and political reform.

For instance, the Proclamation Society began in
1787 as a result of his attempts to soften the savage penal
code. In a letter to Wyvill he observed:

> *The barbarous custom of hanging has been tried too*
> *long, and with the success which might have been*
> *expected from it. The most effectual way to prevent*
> *greater crimes is by punishing the smaller, and by*
> *endeavouring to repress that general spirit of licen-*
> *tiousness, which is the parent of every species of vice.*
> *I know that by regulating the external conduct we do*
> *not at first change the hearts of men, but even they are*
> *ultimately to be wrought upon by these means, and*
> *we should at least so far remove the obtrusiveness of*
> *the temptation, that it may not provoke the appetite,*
> *which might otherwise be dormant and inactive.*[193]

This letter is a fair specimen of Wilberforce's philosophy of social reform. The only way to reduce great
crimes is to eliminate lesser ones. And the best way to
decrease both is to diminish temptation. Though the
heart is not thereby reformed, it is nonetheless educated
and influenced. Moreover, real evil is prohibited. Furneaux notes that this passage summarizes Wilberforce's
"attitude to the problem of vice":

> *Savage punishment was barbarous and futile and it*
> *was far better to remove the opportunities of sin.*
> *The absence of temptation did not mean that a man*
> *would lead a virtuous life, but it would make it easier*
> *for him to do so. The Proclamation Society's object*
> *was to see that laws against Sabbath-breaking, duel-*
> *ling, lotteries, drunkenness, unlicensed entertain-*
> *ment, blasphemy and other unwholesome forms of*
> *behaviour in public were enforced.*[194]

In addition to the Proclamation Society, Wilberforce worked for legal and penal reform. He detested both the savagery of the penal code—hanging a man for poaching a rabbit, for instance—and the barbarity of the prison system. Albeit he did not lead the charge against the rigors of the penal code; yet his voice and vote always supported Romilly, Mackintosh, and other reformers. He frequently lamented "our bloody laws," the "murderous laws," and "the barbarous custom of hanging." In a number of cases he personally intervened to save the lives of young offenders.

Prison conditions were intolerable: filth, brutality, and suffering were common. Often, many inmates were crowded into one room, those guilty of a simple misdemeanor like stealing an apple with those guilty of murder. Eating, sleeping, and defecation all took place in this crowded squalor. Children often accompanied their mothers into prison and were left there until their mothers were released or executed. It was not uncommon to see a child clinging to his mother as she was led to the gallows.[195]

Not surprisingly, Wilberforce supported the work of Elizabeth Fry, Jeremy Bentham, and John Howard. He occasionally accompanied Fry on her missions to Newgate and did much prison visitation on his own initiative. In February 1818 we find him losing sleep over "the two poor women about to be hanged for forgery this day. Alas, how bloody are our laws."[196] He sympathized with the suffering convicts and their families, and gave money out of his own pocket to relieve their hardship.

Wilberforce also supported other legal reforms such as the Factory Acts and Chimney Sweep Bills. Children between the ages of seven and fourteen often worked fourteen hours a day in the mills and factories. Conditions there were oppressively harsh. There were no safety regulations, thus crippling accidents and deaths were not uncommon. Children also worked in gangs in the fields and were employed in coal, tin, and copper mines. The children chimney sweeps were often trapped in chimneys and suffocated to death, or suffered other long-term harm from accidents or the inhalation of soot. Thus, in 1817 and 1819 Wilberforce spoke in favor of the bills to reform the cruel conditions suffered by the chimney sweeps and to improve factory conditions.

Another reform important to Wilberforce was suffrage, or Parliament reform. Members of Commons were elected by "freemen" or "freeholders" in either the county or borough, where qualifications for the franchise varied widely. Rotten boroughs or seats in the Commons were frequently given away (Calthorpe gave Bramber to Wilberforce himself) or bought and sold for influence. It was estimated in 1793 that 51 English and Welsh boroughs, whose total electorate was under 1,500, sent 100 representatives to Commons; whereas 11,075 English and Welsh electors returned only 257 members.[197] Corruption and influence-peddling were widespread, while the populace was not accurately represented in Parliament.

As early as 1786, Wilberforce successfully maneuvered a bill through Commons "aimed directly at purifying county elections by providing a general registration of freeholders and holding the poll in various places at the same time."[198] Yet the Lords killed it. Then war, revolution, and civil unrest postponed any parliamentary reform for many years. In 1809 he supported Curwen's bill making the sale of seats in Parliament illegal, and a year later he voted for Brand's motion to make the representative system "more complete."[199] Only a few days before his death an important parliamentary reform bill passed through both Houses.

# PRUDENCE

*If we cannot stop the whole of this accursed traffic, it is much to stop half of it; and I am resolved to do what I can. . . .*[200]

*W*ILBERFORCE'S SUCCESS AS an abolitionist and reformer was partly a product of a quality rare in men of fixed principles and distant vision. Instead of demanding immediate or total reform, he was able to discern the times in which he lived and steer his causes through the troubled waters of opposition. He understood that to move too quickly or radically would alienate his opponents, thus hindering his ultimate goal. In a word, Wilberforce exercised prudence.

For instance, at the very inception of the Abolition Society, it was debated whether to strive for emancipation or the lesser goal of abolition of the trade. Granville Sharp and others demanded immediate emancipation.

But Wilberforce argued that, of the two, abolition would be easier to achieve, and in the process, the public would be educated on the evils of slavery. Moreover, he hoped that once the trade was abolished the slave owners would of necessity improve their treatment of their slaves. Without a fresh supply of new slaves, they would take better care of the health and lives of the existing ones. As the slaves' lot improved through education, both spiritual and intellectual, they would be encouraged to marry and develop a stable family life. Over time it was hoped that they would become a free peasantry.

This "amelioration" argument, as it was called, turned out to be fallacious, for it assumed that the slave owners would act in a rational manner; that is, in a way that was really in their best interest. But evil is not rational. Once the trade was abolished the owners' treatment of the slaves remained as brutal as before.

Nevertheless, Wilberforce was right in choosing abolition rather than emancipation as the first goal. If he and the abolitionists had moved immediately for emancipation, the opposition would have hardened and the cause would have been set back for years. As it turned out, the entire abolition effort served as a public education campaign on the evils and injustice of slavery itself, and served as the "necessary stepping stone between slavery and freedom."[201] His choice of abolition first was a prudent tactical decision that laid the groundwork for the final goal of total emancipation.

Throughout the campaign Wilberforce had to exercise prudent statesmanship. For instance, as Clarkson traveled England he found many people who had given up sugar as a form of protest. While he initially thought it a good idea, Wilberforce later decided against an official boycott because he thought it would "rouse irritation among the West Indian party and do little good."[202] Also, he was slow to use public petitions for fear that Parliament would view public agitation as revolutionary activity. Only when Parliament proved itself obstinate did he consent to inflame public opinion.[203]

After abolition, Wilberforce moved prudently toward emancipation. When some of the younger abolitionists like T. B. Macaulay and Sir George Stephen wanted to plunge forward and demand total emancipation, Wilberforce advised caution. As events turned out, even Stephen, who was impatient at Wilberforce's "procrastination," had to admit that the introduction of a bill for emancipation in 1823 was premature and that there was no general support for it.[204]

All of Wilberforce's political decisions, not just those related to abolition, reflected the virtue of prudence. For example, after France declared war on England in 1793, Wilberforce mused whether to oppose Pitt's measure to continue the war. With so much at stake, he formed his judgment with due deliberation. "I am making up my mind cautiously and maturely, and therefore slowly," he wrote in 1794, "what is the best course to be observed by Great Britain in the present critical emergency."[205] He chose to oppose his friend.

Likewise, when Wilberforce heard of Pitt's duel with Tierney, he considered presenting a motion in Commons condemning dueling. In response to Pitt's letter asking him not to proceed with the motion, he wrote:

> *I scarcely need assure you that I have given the
> most serious and impartial consideration to the
> question, whether to persist in bringing forward
> my intended motion or to relinquish it. My own
> opinion as to the propriety of it in itself, remains
> unaltered. But being also convinced that it would
> be productive on the whole of more practical harm
> than practical good, and that it would probably
> rather impair than advance the credit of that great
> principle which I wish chiefly to keep in view (I
> mean the duty of obeying the Supreme Being, and cul-
> tivating His favour), I have resolved to give it up. . . .*[206]

Sir James Stephen once said of Wilberforce that "no man ever pursued in Parliament a career more entirely guided by fixed principles." This was because the Scriptures "supplied him with an ordinate by which to measure every curve. They gave him what most public men egregiously want,—the firm hold of a body of unchanging opinions."[207]

Yet he equally had the wisdom to advocate his principles in a judicious and prudent matter. "He was an enthusiast who was always wise."[208] Like other great leaders, he understood that the goal must be kept in view, which meant sometimes rushing forward and other times holding back. It meant compromise, not of principle but of tactic. Wilberforce understood that it is better to attain a partial victory than to suffer a total defeat. Principles must be implemented with prudence.

# ELOQUENCE

*Burke was a great man. Like the fabled object
of the fairies' favours, whenever he opened
his mouth pearls and diamonds dropped
from him.*[209]

*W*ILBERFORCE LIVED DURING THE golden age of political eloquence. In America such renowned
orators as Patrick Henry, Peyton Randolph, and Samuel
Adams enchanted colonial assemblies; while in England Edmund Burke, Richard Sheridan, William Pitt,
and others transfixed the minds of the Commons. The
spoken word determined the fate of nations. This was
the era when rhetoric ruled.

Without question, any member of Parliament who
hoped to be a successful political leader had to master
the art of oratory:

> *Oratory and repartee were both highly regarded arts
> and members expected to be impressed as well as
> convinced. The style of the speaker, the grace of his
> diction and phrases, the facility with which he could
> produce classical allusions to illuminate his theme
> were considered as important as the soundness of
> his arguments. They were the characteristics that
> distinguished an orator from a mere debater. The
> House was responsive, appreciative and stimulat-
> ing when the speaker was good, but merciless to a
> bad one. It was an arena where an individual could
> show his brilliance: oratory there, as well as being
> an art, was a competitive sport.*[210]

Accordingly, Wilberforce diligently labored at
improving his oratorical skills. He attempted to improve
his memory by having a friend read him passages by a distinguished author, which he then repeated back verbatim
if possible. He also studied the classics in order to have a
quiver full of quotations to use in battle. It was Wilberforce's view that some of the best preparation for public
speaking came from sitting on committees and garner-
ing useful facts, and from developing a habit for logical
sequence and elegant writing.

Part of his rhetorical study included an analysis of
the great orators of the day. Of Sheridan he said that "he
came to the House with his flashes prepared and ready
to let off." Fox was indefatigable: "Fox was truly wonderful. He would begin at full tear, and roll on for hours
together without tiring either himself or us." Burke
he greatly admired: "Burke was a great man. I never

could understand how he grew at one time so entirely neglected. In part, undoubtedly it was that, like Mackintosh afterwards, he was above his audience. He had come late into Parliament and had had time to lay in vast stores of knowledge. The field from which he drew his illustrations was magnificent. Like the fable object of the fairies' favours, whenever he opened his mouth pearls and diamonds dropped from him."[211]

Wilberforce's study, preparation, and natural gifts made him a shining star amid this brilliant galaxy. Buxton said that "Wilberforce has more natural eloquence than any of them. . . ." Pitt emphatically agreed, maintaining that "of all the men I ever knew, Wilberforce has the greatest natural eloquence," while Romilly called him "the most efficient speaker in the House of Commons."[212]

After his now famous Castle Yard speech Boswell told Dundas, "I saw a mere shrimp mount on the table; but as I listened, he grew and grew, until the shrimp became a whale"; and High Sheriff Danby said Wilberforce "spoke like an angel."[213] In response to Wilberforce's maiden abolition speech in May of 1789, the celebrated orator Edmund Burke praised his oratory: "The House, the nation, and Europe are under great and serious obligations to the honorable gentleman for having brought forward the subject in a manner the most masterly, impressive, and eloquent. The principles were so well laid down, and supported with so much force and order, that it equalled anything I have ever heard in modern times, and is not perhaps to be surpassed in the remains of Grecian eloquence."[214]

Wilberforce's great weakness as a speaker was his tendency to digress and weigh both sides of any argument. This, at times, made his speeches diffuse. Due to his extremely busy schedule he was not always adequately prepared, either.

But on the other hand, he had the cardinal strengths of a great orator. In addition to important knowledge stored in his memory, the first was his naturally "melodious" voice, a term often applied to it. One auditor remembers, "His voice itself was beautiful; deep, clear, articulate, and flexible,"[215] while another describes his voice as "sweetly musical beyond that of most men, and of great compass."[216]

Second, he had what Sir James Stephen called "unrivalled dramatic powers":

> The student of the history of those times, who shall read some of the discourses which won from him so high a reputation, will scarcely avoid the belief that it was very ill merited. But if he heard them fall from the lips of the speaker—if he had seen him rising with the spirit and self-reliance which Mercutio might have envied, and had listened to those tones so full, liquid, and penetrating, and had watched the eye sparkling as each playful fancy crossed his field of vision, or glowing when he spoke of the oppressions done upon the earth—the fragile form elevating and expanding itself into heroic dignity— and the transitions of his gestures, so rapid and so complete, each successive attitude adapting itself so easily to each new variation of his style—he would

*no more have wondered at the efficacy even of
ordinary topics and of common-place remarks from
such a speaker, than at the magic of the tamest
speech from the lips of Garrick or of Talma.*[217]

Third, Wilberforce was keenly sensitive to the mood
of the House and possessed an acute perception of human
nature. Canning said of Wilberforce, "If there is any one
who understands thoroughly the tactics of debate, and
knows exactly what will carry the House along with him
it is certainly my honorable friend."[218] Wilberforce had,
said another observer, "an intuitive discernment of men,
and a lively sympathy. These enabled him to catch the
temper of the House of Commons. He had learned how
to handle that powerful instrument, which vibrates, like
an organ, to the master's hand, but jars and creaks and
groans when touched by unskillful fingers."[219]

In sum, Wilberforce had "every quality of an orator:
a voice flexible and musical; action easy and effective,
competent knowledge of books, great experience of
human life; the tact which deals with men; a tenacious
memory rich in facts; a fancy stored with images, and the
wit which suggests contrasts."[220]

The importance of proper speech in eighteenth-
century England can hardly be overstated, as may be
gathered from Lord Chesterfield's counsel to his son:
"But in every language, pray attend carefully to the
choice of your words, and to the turn of your expression. Indeed, it is a point of very great consequence. To
be heard with success, you must be heard with pleasure:
words are the dress of thoughts; which should no more

be presented in rags, tatters, and dirt, than your person should."[221]

This is sound advice for all aspiring leaders.

# FAME

*There are some people who spend their whole time and use their utmost endeavour and application in gaining the short-lived and empty praises of a thoughtless and vulgar rabble.*[222]

U NRECOGNIZED GREATNESS IS COMMONPLACE. History is full of examples of poets and prophets, artists and musicians, who go to the grave without fanfare or tribute, to be lauded only many years later.

With Wilberforce, however, it was otherwise. In his own lifetime he was accorded great fame and popularity. Throughout his public career, his reputation grew first as a philanthropist, then as the author of *Practical View,* and last as the champion of the abolition movement. So great was his fame that he has been called "a moral father figure to his country," "the conscience of the nation," and "a legend in his own time."

Stories of his fame are legion. For instance, when Sir Home Popham, cruising off the coast of Haiti, boarded a native ship, the first question he encountered was, "How is Mr. Wilberforce? He is our friend, and benefactor, and we are all interested about him."[223]

Acclamation greeted Wilberforce wherever he went. John Hartford tells the story of when he and Wilberforce went to a public meeting of the Freemasons in Clapham in 1814 to discuss the Peace Treaty and abolition. When they arrived the room was full:

> The proceedings had already commenced. All the leading Members of the Opposition, including Lords Grey, Holland, and Lansdowne, and Messrs Brougham, Tierney etc. were present. There was also a large attendance of those who are mainly prompted by their benevolent feelings. Mr Wilberforce was recognized as soon as he entered the room, and a lane was quickly formed for him to reach the platform. As we advanced, the meeting began to cheer him; for a few moments he was quite unconscious that he himself was the object of applause, for, walking with his head declined upon his breast he saw no one. As he lent on my arm he whispered to me with perfect simplicity, "Have you caught what is going on?" "They seem to me," I replied, "to be all cheering you." The moment he was placed in a conspicuous position the whole room rang for some minutes with repeated thunders of applause.[224]

Scenes like this were frequent. J. C. Colquhoun noted at this time, "In the meetings called from time to time for philanthropic purpose . . . he was the undoubted favourite . . . with characteristic simplicity, he used to wonder at the tumult of applause that greeted his appearance. . . ." In 1818 an Italian visitor to England said of Wilberforce, "When Mr. Wilberforce passes through the crowd on the day of the Opening of Parliament, everyone contemplates this little old man, worn with age and his head sunk upon his shoulders, as a sacred relic, as the Washington of humanity."[225]

When Wilberforce first entered Parliament, his reputation was his darling object. After his conversion, however, he learned that ambition and love of applause were dangerous desires that needed to be mortified. Writing in his *Practical View* he acknowledges their power:

> *The desire of human estimation and distinction, and honour, of the admiration and applause of our fellow creatures, if we take it in its full comprehension, and in all its various modifications, from the thirst of glory to the dread of shame, is the passion of which the empire is by far the most general, and perhaps the authority the most commanding. Though its power be most conspicuous and least controllable in the higher classes of society, it seems, like some resistless conqueror, to spare neither age, nor sex, nor condition. . . . It is often the master passion of the soul.*[226]

Though justified by the world as the parent of noble aspiration, Wilberforce believed that the love of applause was contrary to the teaching of Scripture:

> *But it is undeniably manifest, that in the judgment of the word of God, the love of worldly admiration and applause is in its nature essentially and radically corrupt, so far as it partakes of a disposition to exalt and aggrandize ourselves, or to assume to ourselves the merit and credit of our good qualities, instead of ascribing all the honour and glory where only they are due. . . . It is false, because it exalts that which ought to be abased, and criminal, because it encroaches on the prerogative of God.*[227]

The desire for fame and favor causes one to misconstrue or desert the path of duty. It produces "that quick resentment, those bitter contentions, those angry retorts, those malicious triumphs, that impatience of inferiority, that wakeful sense of past defeats, promptness of revenge. . . ." Worst of all, it has the tendency "to fill us with vain conceits and vicious passions; and above all how it tends to fix the affections on earthly things, and to steal away the heart from God." It is often a veneer for such vices as selfishness, vanity, low ambition, envy and jealousy; detraction, hatred, and variance.[229]

Therefore, the Christian must make it his habit to "set his affections on things above," to "seek heavenly objects," and to make "the love and favour of God" the "matter of our supreme and habitual desire, to which every other should be subordinated. . . ."[230] This is, of course, exactly what Wilberforce did. Throughout his diaries and journals it is clear that whenever he felt the "risings" of ambition, he put it to death by meditating on eternal rewards.

According to Wilberforce, fame should not be sought; but if gained by virtue, it should be used for good. A real man of worth "will studiously and diligently use any degree of worldly credit he may enjoy, in removing or lessening prejudices; in conciliating good-will, and thereby making way for the less obstructed progress of truth. . . . He will make it his business to set on foot and forward benevolent and useful schemes. . . . He will endeavour to discountenance vice, to bring modest merit into notice. . . ." And in sum, he will make his good reputation "subservient to the great end of advancing the cause of Religion and Virtue, and of promoting the happiness and comfort of mankind. . . ."[231]

Fame thus used is truly deserved.

# HUMILITY

*Humility is indeed the vital principle of
Christianity; that principle by which from
first to last she lives and thrives, and in
proportion to the growth or decline of
which she must decay or flourish.*[232]

WILBERFORCE WAS NOT CORRUPTED by his popularity because he possessed genuine humility, a
rare trait in men otherwise great. In fact, it is often a
man's greatness, or at least his great accomplishments or
gifts, which make him susceptible to pride. If the virtue
of humility is not assiduously cultivated, the noblest
leader can succumb to this deadly vice—"for pride
cometh before a fall."

According to Wilberforce the only antidote to the
innate desire for human applause is for Christians to exercise "a laborious watchfulness, a jealous guard, a close
and frequent scrutiny of their own hearts, that they may

not mistake their real character. . . ." By God's grace, true Christians should "fix in themselves a deep, habitual, and practical sense of the excellence of 'that honour which cometh from God,' and of the comparative worthlessness of all earthly estimation and pre-eminence."[233] As is evidenced from his diaries and journals, Wilberforce practiced a daily watchfulness and self-inspection.

Most significantly, humility is cultivated when we look to Christ and his cross, and there determine our real condition. Writing in *Practical View* Wilberforce says:

> *He was meek and lowly of heart, and from the study of his character we shall best learn the lessons of humility. Contemplating the work of Redemption, we become more and more impressed with the sense of our natural darkness, and helplessness, and misery, from which it was requisite to ransom us at such a price; more and more conscious that we are utterly unworthy of all the amazing condescension and love which have been manifested towards us; ashamed of the callousness of our tenderest sensibility, and of the poor returns of our most active services.*[234]

Contemplating the cross has salutary and humbling effects:

> *Considerations like these, abating our pride and reducing our opinion of ourselves, naturally moderate our pretension towards others. We become less disposed to exact that respect for our persons, and*

> *that deference for our authority, which we naturally covet; we less sensibly feel a slight, and less hotly resent it; we grow less irritable, less prone to be dissatisfied, more soft, and meek, and courteous, and placable, and condescending. . . . At the same time the Holy Scriptures assuring us, that to the powerful operations of the Holy Spirit, purchased for us by the death of Christ, we must be indebted for the success of all our endeavours after improvement in virtue; the conviction of this truth tends to render us diffident of our own powers, and to suppress the first risings of vanity.*[235]

Wilberforce's humility was demonstrated on many occasions. When he was considering retirement from Parliament he struggled with a sense of having achieved so little after many years in Commons. Writing to his friend Hartford, he lamented:

> *When I consider that my public life is nearly expired, and when I review the many years I have been in it, I am filled with the deepest compunction, from the consciousness of my having made so poor a use of the talents committed to my stewardship. The heart knows its own bitterness. We alone know ourselves, the opportunities we have enjoyed, the comparative use we have made of them. But it is only to your friendly ear that I breathe out my secret sorrow. I might be supposed by others to be fishing for a compliment. Well, it is an unspeakable consolation that we*

> *serve a gracious Master who giveth liberally and*
> *upbraideth not.*[236]

For sentiments such as these to come from Wilberforce after all he had accomplished—the abolition of
the slave trade, the Proclamation Society, educational
projects, philanthropic enterprises, penal reform, legal
reform, the list goes on—for a man who had his hand
in more than fifty organizations designed to benefit his
fellow man, not to mention his "regular" work as an
M.P.—for such a man to lament his lack of usefulness is
surely a profound statement of humility.

Yet Wilberforce meant it. When Sir John Sinclair suggested Wilberforce be made a peer so he could engage in
public life without the work of Commons, he declared
that he had not deserved it: "As I had done nothing to
make it naturally come to me, I must have endeavoured
to go to it; and this would have been carving from myself,
if I may use the expression, much more than a Christian
ought to do."[237]

Wilberforce's years in retirement are described by
Hartford: "No cares, no repinings appear to have any
place in his mind. Instead of recurring to the great part
which he has acted in public life with self-complacency
or appearing desirous of fixing attention upon himself,
his whole deportment bespeaks an entire self-renuncia-
tion—a deep and unfeigned humility. . . ."[238] Near the
end of his life, the man who spent his life to establish
justice, encourage morality, and alleviate the suffering of
his fellow men—the man who spared millions from deg-

radation and bondage—could only say, "I am sadly an unprofitable servant."[239]

On the evening of his death, in an interval of consciousness, he said to his son Henry, "I am in a very distressed state." "Yes," his son responded, "but you have your feet on the Rock." To which Wilberforce replied, "I do not venture to speak so positively, but I hope I have."[240]

His very last words were a testimony to his humility.

# POWER

*It is a striking instance of the way in which
Providence, to show the inutility of human
rank, power and even talents, when it has a
great design to execute selects some mean and
apparently, inefficient instrument.*[241]

*T*HERE ARE THREE TYPES OF POWER: the power that
comes from status, the power that comes from
talent, and the power that comes from character. Wilberforce had all three.

Early in his political career Wilberforce had the
power that came from being financially secure—or independently wealthy, we might say. But this was merely
the power of doing as he pleased. It was not in any real
sense power over other men. When he captured Yorkshire, one of the two most influential seats in Commons,

his power increased. And, in addition, Wilberforce's friendship with Prime Minister Pitt gave him an influence unavailable to many of his colleagues.

Wilberforce also possessed the power that came from his natural and cultivated gifts. His charm was winning and disarming, thus being one of his most potent weapons. And when wedded to his rhetoric, his power over others was almost irresistible, which is why Canning said, in essence, that he could move the House in any direction he desired.

In 1807, when he emerged victorious from both the abolition campaign and the polls, his prestige in England was virtually unparalleled. He was now considered "the conscience of the nation." As Cormack put it:

> His standing in the country and in Parliament was quite unique. No man before, and no one since, has held quite his position. Unconnected to any great family, belonging to no party or faction, holding no office or official position, he was yet regarded by all as among the foremost men of his time, and by many in Parliament and outside as the living embodiment of the national conscience.[242]

The key to Wilberforce's power was the reputation he earned, and deserved, for philanthropy and character. And in the eyes of many, these two were inseparable. In a word, Wilberforce possessed "moral authority," or the power of a virtuous character. James Stephen said that in Commons, "any one speaks with immense advantage whose character, station, or presumed knowledge is such as to give importance to his opinions. The dogmas of some men are of incomparably more value there than the logic of others; and no member, except the leaders of the great contending parties, addressed the House with an authority equal to that of Mr. Wilberforce." Why? Because "the homage rendered to his personal character, his command over a small but compact party, his representation of the county of York, the confidence of the great religious bodies in every part of England, and, above all, his independent neutrality, gave to his suffrage an almost unexampled value."[243]

Wilberforce's reputation for virtue and integrity was unmatched. Colquhoun said:

> *Wilberforce had a religious norm of conduct to which he felt he had to conform. But others judged him differently. They, as they watched him, could scarcely believe that human worth could reach so rare perfection. Spirits so buoyant, and yet so self-restrained; a temper so cheerful, yet so even; wit so playful, and yet so innocent; perfection so expansive, and yet so true; a courtesy so uniform, a thoughtfulness so considerate; such reverence for the will of God, yet such charity for man.*[244]

Lord Teignmouth used to tell a story that illustrates the power of Wilberforce's name. Once, when he and Wilberforce were visiting Bath, they spied two men who were cruelly driving their horses up a steep street when one of them fell. The carter, who was a giant burly man, began to beat the horse mercilessly "mingled with hoarse curses." Wilberforce "rushed forward when the giant had raised his hand for a further blow, and interfered, pouring upon him at the same time a torrent of eloquent rebuke":

> *The fellow arrested in the very height of passion, and furious at the language used, stood with his face like a thundercloud, as if meditating to turn his stroke on the puny elf who appeared before him. At this moment his companion, who had recognized Wilberforce, stepped up to him and whispered his name. The word acted like a charm. In an instant the lowering face cleared, and from rage and sullen hatred the look passed at once into wondering reverence as if, in the midst of his brutal passions and debasement, there was suddenly presented to him an object that awakened the better feelings of his nature, and drew forth his slumbering sympathies.*[245]

According to Wilberforce, social rank meant little. All men were created by God and were equal in his eyes. To "look down with contempt" on those of lower birth was "contrary to the precept of Scriptures to 'condescend to men of low estate,'" he once wrote to Samuel.[246]

If Lord Acton's axiom—"power corrupts, and absolute power corrupts absolutely"—is a general rule, then Wilberforce is the exception. Never in his entire political career did he use his power for personal gain. And not once did he exploit his friendship with Pitt for his own advantage. Rather, he always used his political power and personal influence to advance religion, morality, and his humanitarian causes. In fact, it was his opinion that wealth and power were privileges that brought moral obligations— *noblesse oblige.* His advice to all who aspire to power would be this:

> *In whatever class or order of society Christianity prevails, she sets herself to rectify the particular faults, or, if we would speak more distinctly, to counteract the particular mode of selfishness, to which that class is liable. Affluence she teaches to be liberal and beneficent; authority, to bear its faculties with meekness, and to consider the various cares and obligations belonging to its elevated station as being conditions on which that station is conferred.*[247]

# PERSEVERANCE

*Our motto must continue to be perseverance.
And ultimately I trust the Almighty will crown
our efforts with success.*[248]

*T*HE DIFFERENCE BETWEEN a dreamer's wish and a
leader's accomplishment is often nothing more
glamorous than plodding perseverance: the determination to continue working for the goal in spite of obstacles
and setbacks; the will to win in the face of defeat and
disappointment; the passion to press on when discouraged or discounted.

The leader who tenaciously pursues his objective is
usually victorious over the man who may be more intel-
ligent or more gifted. As in Aesop's fable of the tortoise
and the hare, perseverance wins the prize.

When Wilberforce entered Parliament at the tender age of twenty-one, he was ignorant of his true calling in life. Like so many of his political colleagues, he saw his office as a means to personal advancement. However, in 1784–85, he traveled Europe with his mother, sister, and former schoolmaster Isaac Milner. To pass the time, Wilberforce and Milner read Phillip Doddridge's classic, *The Rise and Progress of Religion in the Soul,* and discussed the New Testament as they rode together in the coach. After a season of conviction and anguish, Wilberforce was converted.

For the next few years he struggled with his vocation. What was God's will for him? Could he be both a worldly politician and a pious Christian? In desperation he visited the now famous clergyman John Newton, who counseled him to stay in politics, believing that perhaps God would use him in that arena. Providentially, it was Newton, along with James Ramsay, Thomas Clarkson, and others, who influenced Wilberforce to take up the cause of the slaves.

In 1787, as Wilberforce wrestled with God, he penned in his diary the conviction that God had called him to labor for the abolition of the slave trade. In light of his divine call, as well as the self-evident righteousness of his cause, Wilberforce expected a quick and easy victory. But he could not have been any more mistaken: "The pathway to abolition was fraught with difficulty. Vested interest, parliamentary filibustering, entrenched bigotry, international politics, slave unrest, personal sickness, and political fear—all combined to frustrate the move-

ment."[249] Little did he know it would take twenty long
and hard years of persistent effort to see his hope fulfilled.

Wilberforce began to press in Parliament the claims
of the slaves in 1787. A year later, however, he fell seriously ill and had to postpone his efforts for a year. By
1789 he recuperated, and issued his first parliamentary
speech for abolishing the wicked trade. "I trust . . . I have
proved that, upon every ground, total abolition ought to
take place," he told Parliament. And even though, backed
by Burke, Pitt, and others, the issue was deferred until
next session, Parliament agreeing to have the question
considered under committee. Not until 1791 did the
committee finish its work, yet Wilberforce was again
defeated 88 to 163. Further demoralizing defeats followed in 1792 and 1793.

Then came war with France in February 1793, which
had the effect of relegating the abolition of the slave trade
into a measure of minor importance. Though he tried a
new tactic of bringing forward a bill (the Foreign Slave
Bill) to prohibit the carrying of slaves to foreign shores in
British ships, Wilberforce was again defeated—this time
by two votes. For the next fourteen years he persevered
in the fight but was repeatedly beaten: in 1796 (70 to
74), in 1797 (74 to 82), in 1798 (83 to 87), and in 1799
(54 to 84). It was not until 1804 that Wilberforce won
a victory in Commons, only to be overthrown in the
House of Lords.

While continual defeats might have crushed a
leader of less perseverance and determination, Wilberforce maintained a confident tenacity borne of his deep

religious faith. As far back as 1793 he expressed a firm determination to complete what he had begun:

> *In the case of every question of political expediency there appears to me room for consideration of times and seasons. . . . But in the present instance where the actual commission of guilt is in question, a man who fears God is not at liberty. . . . Be persuaded then, I shall still even less make this grand cause the sport of caprice, or sacrifice it to motives of political convenience or personal feeling.*[250]

After another defeat in 1805, a clerk of the Commons suggested he give up the fight. Wilberforce rebuffed him: "I do expect to carry it," he insisted, "and what is more, I feel assured that I shall carry it speedily."[251] In the face of defeat, Wilberforce smelled the scent of victory—and he was right. The following year (1806) Parliament finally passed a bill prohibiting the "importation of slaves by British ships into Colonies annexed by Britain during the war, or into any Colonies of a foreign State, and to prohibit the outfitting of foreign slave ships in British ports, or the employment of British capital or labour therein."[252] The measure became law, and at long last the enemy was on the run.

A year later the Bill for the Abolition of the Slave Trade was introduced to Parliament. On February 23, 1807, abolition was secured by a vote of 287 to 16. And as the attorney general, Sir Samuel Romilly, stood and praised the perseverance of Wilberforce, the House rose to its feet and broke out in cheers. Wilberforce was so overcome with emotion that he sat head in hand, tears streaming down his face.

Astonishingly, Wilberforce did not rest satisfied with his victory; for although the trade was now legally abolished, there were still men in chains. So he again took up the cause of the slaves, and again had to exercise an almost supernatural perseverance as he now pushed for the total abolition of slavery. In spite of personal criticism, threats on his life, and deep-seated prejudice on the part of many colleagues, Wilberforce labored for an additional twenty-six years until, on July 26, 1833, the Emancipation Bill passed through Parliament. Three days later, Wilberforce died.

Perseverance had won the prize.

# PART III
## THE LEGACY OF
## WILLIAM WILBERFORCE

*Happy was it for his contemporaries and for posterity that he did not retire into ascetic solitude, but that he devoted his rare gifts to his friends, to his country, and to the world, and showed by his example how a Christian may leaven society, and influence the whole tone of legislation and public life.*[1]

*Considering the enormous difficulties of the undertaking, and how nearly impossible it is to persuade large bodies of men to give up ancient sins—sins which have been patronized and protected for centuries—sins which are profitable and "respectable,"—we may now look back with astonishment on the success granted to William Wilberforce. . . .*[2]

*But woe to them whose joy is in the invasion of great names, and in the overthrow of great reputations.*[3]

# THE WILBERFORCE ENIGMA

*W*ILBERFORCE'S REPUTATION as a philanthropist and statesman has suffered from what has been called "the Wilberforce enigma." Biographer Robin Furneaux put it like this:

> The contrast between Wilberforce's passionate support for freedom for the slaves and his opposition to his countrymen's efforts to achieve freedom has jarred on many of those who have written about him. It has been called "the Wilberforce enigma." He has, not unnaturally, been accused of hypocrisy and double standards, most notably in Hazlitt's essay on him, which declared: "His patriotism, his philanthropy are not so ill bred, as to quarrel with his loyalty to or banish him from the first circles. He preaches vital Christianity to untutored savages; and tolerates its worst abuses in civilised states."[4]

The charge that Wilberforce opposed his countrymen's freedom is based on his support of several government measures that had the effect of limiting constitutional liberties. Consider the following evidence.

First there were the bills against treasonable and seditious meetings. In 1794, shortly after England went to war against France, there was a series of bad harvests. Scarcity, enclosures, wartime hardship, and inadequate relief for the poor led to radical Jacobin agitation. After the king had his carriage mobbed, Parliament responded with the suspension of habeus corpus. Political meetings were limited, and any seditious speeches were grounds for immediate arrest.

Then there was the prosecution of the bookseller Williams in 1797. Thomas Williams was a poor bookseller who had published Paine's *Age of Reason*,[5] and was duly prosecuted by the Proclamation Society. The trial took place in June, and in April of 1798 Williams was sentenced to one year hard labor and then had to post bond of one thousand pounds. Years later, in 1821, Mary Ann Carlile was prosecuted for publishing *An Appendix to Thomas Paine's Age of Reason*. She was fined and sent to prison for a year.

Next came the Combination Act. In April of 1799 the master millwrights presented a petition to Commons against a trade union that had been formed by their journeymen. Instead of supporting the particular petition, Wilberforce suggested a general law against "combinations," or what we today would call trade unions. The law, which passed Parliament in June, severely curtailed the rights of the working poor. Fortunately, a year later some of its more onerous features were repealed.

Finally, there were the Six Acts. The years 1816 to 1820 were some of the bleakest in England's history. Bad harvests left the economy in a deep slump. The poor were truly suffering. When the radicals again began agitation, Parliament, with Wilberforce's support, passed a series of laws that again suspended habeas corpus and imposed other limitations on the people's liberties.

So, how do we account for this apparent anomaly of Wilberforce—the champion of liberty—supporting meas-ures that were repressive? What is the answer to the enigma?

The answer, it appears, lies partly in the British reaction to events in France. It is very difficult for us today to appreciate the profound impact that the French Revolution had on the upper classes in England. One has only to read Burke's treatment of that volcanic event to see what a majority of those in Parliament thought of the French Revolution.[6] It was not viewed as a foreign affair at all; it was seen as a poison that was already infecting British society. Fear of the guillotine was real. Insurrection and bloodshed seemed immanent. Thus, when the Jacobins or other social radicals held public meetings or organized marches, the government (including Wilberforce) expected the worst.

Since an outright revolution never occurred, however, the government's fear seems, in hindsight, to have been unfounded; which makes its measures appear all the more repressive. Yet we must judge the government's response by what seemed reasonable at the time, not by what we know from subsequent history. By all appearances, the threat of revolution was real. "The grim figure of the Jacobin brooded over every debate."[7]

Additionally, for Wilberforce the threat may have seemed even more serious because of his religious faith. He believed in the judgment of God on men and nations, and as Wilberforce surveyed the moral landscape, especially of the upper classes, he was appalled at the moral squalor. How long would God tolerate such gross abuses of privilege and power? How long would he wink at the gambling, the gluttony, the drunkenness, and the adultery? How long would he stay his hand of judgment on such selfish arrogance and venal pride? Even more significantly, how long would God tolerate the abomination of slavery before sending retribution? Certainly not forever. And Wilberforce feared that revolution, or perhaps defeat by France, might be God's chosen instrument of vengeance. "Is not this a time," he said during the height of war and unrest, "in which all who believe in the superintending providence of God must feel desirous of averting His displeasure?"[8]

Moreover, because eighteenth-century radicalism was deeply tinctured with atheism, Wilberforce saw it as a threat to social stability. His support for suppressing Paine's writings, which were intentionally provocative and inflammatory, can be attributed to his disgust of blasphemy and his fear that atheism, under the guise of Jacobinism, was shaking the foundations of society— even threatening the British constitution itself. While such censorship would be unthinkable today, it was not uncommon in Wilberforce's day, especially in a country that had an established church. Wilberforce was conservative but not reactionary.

It must be added that regarding the suspension of habeas corpus or other constitutional liberties, Wilberforce only envisioned a temporary suspension during times of crisis. Moreover, the right to petition Parliament and the freedom of the press were left untouched, and he saw these liberties as a safeguard for the people. His opposition to trade unions, or "combinations" must be understood as a general suspicion of radicalism, and not as a direct attempt to oppress the poor.

Finally, we must keep in mind that the only reason there is even an "enigma" to discuss is because Wilberforce was, in many respects, a man ahead of his time. This was certainly the case with abolition, as well as many other reforms. Yet no man is ever ahead of his time in every respect. To judge Wilberforce's domestic record by today's "progressive" perspective is not wholly fair. The accomplishments of any great man must be measured in light of what preceded him, not by what others have done after him.

Likewise, Wilberforce's accomplishments must be viewed in the historical context in which he lived. He was certainly not a perfect man, nor was he free from every assumption and perspective of his age. Yet despite his errors and shortcomings, he was a truly remarkable man whose life and labors helped eradicate one of humankind's longest and most wicked evils.

# THE WORLD'S BENEFACTOR

*I*N 1919 A TABLET WAS BUILT into the south wall of the Clapham parish church with the following inscription:

## LET US PRAISE GOD

For the memory and example of all the faithful departed who have worshipped in this Church, and especially for the under named Servants of Christ sometime called

### THE CLAPHAM SECT

Who in the latter part of the XVIIIth and early part of the XIXth Centuries laboured so abundantly for the increase of National Righteousness and the Conversion of the Heathen, and rested not until the curse of slavery was swept away from all parts of the British Dominions—

| | |
|---|---|
| Charles Grant | John Thornton |
| Zachary Macaulay | Henry Venn |

Granville Sharp            (Curate of Clapham)
John Shore                 John Venn
(Lord Teignmouth)          (Rector of Clapham)
James Stephen              William Wilberforce
                Henry Thornton

"O God, we have heard with our ears, and our fathers
have declared unto us, the noble works that Thou didst
in their days, and in the old time before them."

When one looks around the Clapham Common it
is shocking to see that Thornton's house has been lev-
eled and little remains to remind us of the heroic life and
deeds of Wilberforce and the Saints. Yet perhaps that is
as it should be; for the legacy left by Wilberforce tran-
scends any particular locale. He was the world's benefactor. Like other great leaders he not only made a mark on
his own time and place, but he also made an indelible
mark on future generations throughout the world.

Wilberforce's most obvious legacy is the contribution he made to human liberty. At midnight on July 31,
1834, just one year after his death, eight hundred thousand slaves in the British Dominions were set free. This
was "more than a great event in African or in British
history. It was one of the greatest events in the history
of mankind."[9] Indeed, it was. For not only were those
slaves freed, but millions more Africans escaped the
bondage that would have been their fate had not Wilberforce and the Saints labored to abolish the trade and then
emancipate the slaves. Their tireless pressure on foreign

powers guaranteed the eventual death of slavery in the entire West, excluding the United States, which had to endure the crucible of civil war to cleanse away the evil.

Black persons around the world owe a debt of gratitude to Wilberforce for the liberty they now enjoy. As Dean Inge has noted, "It is terrible to reflect what might have happened if slavery had not been abolished before the partition of Africa among the Great Powers. The whole of the Dark Continent might have become a gigantic slave farm, with consequences to the social and economic condition of Europe itself which cannot be calculated."[10] Historian G. M. Trevelyan agrees: "On the last night of slavery . . . far away in the forest of Central Africa, in the heart of darkness yet unexplored, none understood or regarded the day. Before its exploitation by Europe had well begun, the most powerful of the nations that were to control its destiny had decided that slavery should not be the relation of the black man to the white."[11]

Wilberforce's legacy can also be seen in the continent of India. When he labored on the East India Bill the relation between the two countries was one of "soulless exploitation on the one side" and "servile hate and fear" on the other. Yet Wilberforce and the Saints changed all that. They impressed upon Commons the ideals of trusteeship: economic intercourse involved moral obligations. By opening the doors of India to missionaries, they not only helped to ameliorate the brutality of certain Hindu customs, they also provided an advocate class for the native people. As one historian has observed, "It was the influence of the missionaries which was to establish the principle that, in the backward regions of the world, it was the duty of the British power to prevent the ruthless exploitation of primitive peoples, and to lead them gently into civilized ways of life."[12]

Wilberforce has also left a legacy of political reform. When he entered Commons, Parliament was a club of wealthy men whose main objective was to look after and advance their own interests. Corruption and privilege were deeply rooted in both Houses. Influence was traded for favors. Sinecure was for sale. But Wilberforce and the Saints, although a minority, transformed the way Parliament did business. They took into Commons the principles that governed them in their private life. Wilberforce, Thornton, Babington, and others stayed in Parliament for many years without taking a bribe or suffering an electoral defeat. As a result, they gained a moral ascendancy in the House that gave them an influence beyond their numbers, and that helped to reform the character of British politics. One of their legacies, therefore, was "their undoubted share in the improvement of our [British] political integrity."[13] The impact of Wilberforce on Parliament can be seen by noting that at the beginning of his career in 1787 there were only three known Christians sitting in Parliament; yet by the end of his life more than one hundred members of the House of Commons and another one hundred members of the House of Lords were committed Christians.[14]

Social reform was another of Wilberforce's legacies. Through his efforts at educational reform, penal reform, legislative reform, as well as his numerous charitable organizations outside of Parliament, he helped improve the spiritual, moral, and physical condition of millions of his countrymen. In one five-year period alone, the Society for the Relief of Debtors obtained the release of fourteen thousand people from prison. When we think of the myriad of humanitarian enterprises that Wilberforce supported in one way or another, his influence is nearly incalculable. In the generation that followed Wilberforce's death, Lord Shaftesbury, "the Wilberforce of the whites," undertook a campaign for the "factory-slaves" that transformed working conditions. Howse rightly notes that "under Wilberforce and Shaftesbury the Evangelicals left to England a legacy of extraordinary social achievements."[15]

Last, Wilberforce left the legacy of his personal example. Due to his influence, morality and religion were restored to a place of respectability. Victorian optimism and social action followed in his wake. Many people now believed that evil could be fought and conquered. As Sir James Mackintosh said in 1807, shortly after the triumph of abolition, "Who knows whether the greater part of the benefit that he has conferred on the world . . . may not be the encouraging example that the exertions of virtue may be crowned by such splendid success? . . . Hundreds and thousands will be animated by Mr. Wilberforce's example . . . to attack all forms of corruption and cruelty that scourge mankind."[16]

In the generation that followed his death, many labored against evil under the banner of Wilberforce's example. May it be so once again.

# THE WASHINGTON OF HUMANITY

*W*ILBERFORCE WAS ONCE DESCRIBED as "the Washington of humanity," which meant, among other things, that he was a model of moral virtue and Christian statesmanship. He was a man who could not be corrupted by wealth, fame, or power. His character was his armor.

So what can Wilberforce, the model, teach today's leaders?

First, we can learn the importance of religious faith. Everything he was as a person, and everything he accomplished as a leader, was an expression of his Christian faith. And any attempt to "secularize" the abolition movement in Britain is a revision of history. That anyone could study Wilberforce's life and come to the conclusion that his Christian faith was not his predominant motive, surely demonstrates the degree to which historical studies have been vitiated by political correctness and degraded by secular assumptions. It requires a monumental intellectual effort not to see the obvious. Yet, as Gertrude Himmelfarb has rightly said: "An ingenious historian can always find ways of eluding reality."[17] Unfortunately, some historians are driven more by political ideology than by a concern for historical truth.

Whatever interest Wilberforce might have had in abolition before his conversion, it is clear from the record that instead of being a man who found a cause, he was a man who felt called by God. Those immortal words penned in his diary say it all: "*God Almighty* has set before me. . . ." Wilberforce believed that God had called him to the task of abolition, and it was this Christian conviction that sustained him during the long and arduous struggle. Moreover, he and the Saints felt it was their Christian duty to alleviate the suffering, and rectify the injustices, of their world. They were not humanistic "do-gooders," they were Christian activists. As the term "Saints" suggests, their faith in Christ was central to all their humanitarian schemes.

Second, Wilberforce teaches us the necessity of integrity. He was a man who was both a Christian and a politician, and the two were genuinely "integrated." Wilberforce did not subscribe to the notion, popular both then and now, that faith and politics do not mix, or that a politician should keep his religious views separate from his public policies. He did not accept a dichotomy between the secular and the sacred. The question we have to ask ourselves is this: If a man is not governed by his private views, then by what is he governed? Popular opinion? Party affiliation? The love of applause? The quest for fame? Is it any wonder we today lack states-men of Wilberforce's stature when we tell our politicians to act on some principle other than what they really believe? We cut out their souls and demand greatness. Or, as C. S. Lewis put it, "we castrate and bid the geld-ings be fruitful."[18]

Third, because Wilberforce did not divorce his faith from his calling, he was a principled politician. In fact, perhaps the best way to define the difference between a mere politician and a true statesman is to say that the latter governs according to principles that transcend the personal or the political. Wilberforce did not govern by policy or by party; he governed by principle. And his principles were the eternal truths he found in God's Word. This produced a statesman who was tenacious in his pursuit of justice, indefatigable in his work of char-ity, and, most important, impervious to the corruption of power or fame.

Much of Wilberforce's success as a statesman and reformer was due to his reputation for virtue. It was not that he simply held the right principles. He actually lived them. He not only governed by principle; principle gov-erned him. People learned that Wilberforce was genu-inely altruistic and truly good, and such a principled life won him trust, affection, and respect.

Fourth, Wilberforce was a realistic, or practical, reformer. While exercising visionary leadership, he never got lost in ideals or abstractions. That is why he was a reformer and not a revolutionary, and a humanitarian but not a utopian. Like Burke, he abhorred the French Revolution and the "ideals" that unleashed its fury. The lesson from France was that, in reference to reform, philosophical abstraction leads to societal destruction. He also did not fall into the utopian error of thinking that changing "institutions" or "structures" was the solution to mankind's ills. Yes, he worked for parliamentary reform, penal reform, and other types of reform. But the foundation of his hope for lasting and deep reform lay in genuine spiritual conversion. That is why he penned *Practical View,* and why he supported various Bible societies, Christian schools, and mission projects. Wilberforce was in the business of reforming souls.

He did not, however, make the mistake—so common today—of adopting the "either-or" philosophy. He did not believe that since legislation does not transform the heart at the deepest level, therefore it is useless; nor did he believe that evangelism alone was sufficient. The answer to vice was not "either-or," it was both. While holding that Christianity secured "the foundations of the social edifice," he also held that there was a legitimate place for suppressing vice through legislation.[19] Abolition is a prime example. While the Great Awakening played an important part in changing attitudes toward slavery, thus providing a powerful force in the form of public opinion, the slave trade and slavery itself were abolished by law—despite the protests of owners and planters.

Fifth, Wilberforce was a leader filled with deep compassion. Reformers can be a dangerous breed because their "righteous" indignation can easily and unwittingly devolve into a dark and bitter hatred. And any movement built on bitterness is bound to yield bitter fruit. Again, the French Revolution provides a fitting illustration. History is replete with examples of real people being sacrificed on the altar of "humanity" or some other "noble" ideal by reformers who are fueled, not by a genuine love of their fellow man, but by their hatred of "oppression" or "injustice." Wilberforce avoided the dark side of reform because he was motivated by a sincere love of his fellow man. He was unquestionably angry at the inhumanity and injustice of the slave trade, for instance, but he never let his indignation turn into a hatred of persons. He loved both the oppressor and the oppressed. Because "God so loved the world," so did he.

Finally, Wilberforce was a leader with profound perseverance. It is easy to adopt the false notion that because something *did* happen it was *bound* to happen—as if history runs on a fixed course regardless of personal decisions. This is, of course, the erroneous idea of historical necessity. Looking back on Wilberforce's crusade against abolition through the eyes of historical necessity is to minimize his accomplishment. We must remember that there was no guarantee of success; there was no assurance of victory; there was no fate that predetermined the outcome. If Wilberforce had not made the decision to undertake abolition, and if he had not persevered in his course, then abolition would not have occurred when it did. Though some historians have argued that slavery would have eventually been abolished or would have "died out" because of increasing industrialization, the historical fact is this: abolition and emancipation throughout the British Empire took place when it did because of the perseverance of Wilberforce and the Saints. He fought an upward battle against powerful and hostile opposition; he was not riding along on a pleasant wave of historical necessity.

It is people, and especially leaders, rather than impersonal causes, who are the prime determinants in human history:

> *It is the fashion of some contemporary historians to minimize the significance of moral factors in history; to conclude that regardless of such men as Woolman and Wilberforce, Livingstone and Lincoln, slavery would have disappeared anyway; and, indeed, that the errors of each generation of the past have been inexorably outmoded by the impersonal working of material forces. Such thinking is the vestigial remnant of a romanticism now sadly discredited, and its dangerous unreality has been made clear by contemporary experience. Nothing in human history promises that evil will ever be eliminated without toil, pain, and vicarious suffering, or without the inspiration of men animated by the noble insights of religion.*[20]

Because of his supernatural perseverance, as well as his many other virtues, Wilberforce was a leader who positively affected the lives of millions of people and shaped the history of Western civilization. Therefore, he deserves our admiration and emulation. A sentence from Swift's epitaph speaks poignantly of Wilberforce, and may be taken as an exhortation to all who aspire to transformational leadership: "Imitate him if you can; he served the cause of human liberty."

# PART IV
## WILLIAM WILBERFORCE
## THE LESSONS OF LEADERSHIP

- Providence prepares the path of every great leader.
- A leader's religious faith is inseparable from his worldly accomplishments.
- Since true leadership entails integrity, what a leader says and does must be one.
- A wise leader will acknowledge his faults and welcome the criticism of his friends.
- If a leader would improve the world he must first improve himself.
- No one respects ignorance; a leader must read in order to gain wisdom and knowledge.
- A leader expands his influence by being kind and winsome.
- Since a man's friends shape his thought and life, a leader must choose friends wisely.
- A leader must have the gravitational force that draws men together for teamwork.
- A leader who truly loves God will also love his fellow man.
- Private benevolence says more about a leader's character than public charity.
- A large capacity for work is the earmark of a world-class leader.

❧ A day of rest is the springboard for a week of labor.

❧ A Christian leader will never forget that his colleagues have an eternal destiny.

❧ A leader who has embraced the gospel will support its spread worldwide.

❧ A leader will do his duty even if it means standing alone.

❧ Principled leadership means being governed by principles that transcend the personal or political.

❧ A life well lived is the best answer to criticism undeserved.

❧ The advantages of leadership are no shield from the adversities of life.

❧ Before he can govern others, a leader must first govern himself.

❧ A leader must choose a virtuous and compatible wife.

❧ A good leader should equally be a good father and husband.

❧ Mere visionaries are many; men of vision are rare.

❧ Principled and visionary leadership makes a leader a reformer.

❧ A wise leader advocates his cause in a judicious and prudent manner; he is neither radical nor reactionary.

❧ To be heard with success, a leader must be heard with pleasure.

❧ Fame is truly deserved when it is used to advance morality and religion.

❧ The noblest leader may succumb to pride if he does not cultivate humility.

❧ The benefits of leadership bring the moral obligation to benefit others.

❧ Perseverance wins the prize.

# NOTES

## FOREWORD

1. Thomas Chalmers, *Essays and Speeches,* (Edinburgh: William Collins, 1846), 171.
2. Ibid., 174.
3. Ibid.
4. Kenneth Meyers, *All God's Children Wear Blue Suede Shoes,* (Wheaton, Ill.: Crossway, 1989), xi.
5. *World,* May 14, 1992.
6. Eugene Peterson, *A Long Obedience in the Same Direction,* (Downers Grove, Ill.: IVP, 1986).

### PART I: THE LIFE OF WILLIAM WILBERFORCE

1. James Stephen, *Essays in Ecclesiastical Biography,* vol. 2 (London: Longman, Brown, Green, and Longmans, 1850), 203.
2. Ernest Marshall Howse, *Saints in Politics: The Clapham Sect and the Growth of Freedom* (Toronto: University of Toronto Press, 1952), viii.
3. Gerard Edwards in Garth Lean, *God's Politician: William Wilberforce's Struggle* (Colorado Springs: Helmer & Howard, 1987), 19.
4. W. E. H. Lecky, *History of European Morals,* vol. 1 (1869; reprint, New York: George Braziller, 1955), 236–37.
5. Revelation 22:17, author's translation.

6. Reginald Coupland, *The British Anti-Slavery Movement* (London: Frank Cass & Co., 1964), 9–10; hereafter, *BASM*.

7. Robin Furneaux, *William Wilberforce* (London: Hamish Hamilton, 1974), 61.

8. Reginald Coupland, *Wilberforce* (1923; reprint, London: Collins, 1945), 68.

9. James Boswell, *The Life of Samuel Johnson* (New York: Modern Library, 1932), 364.

10. Coupland, *Wilberforce*, 77–78.

11. John Charles Pollock, *Wilberforce* (New York: St. Martin's Press 1977), 6.

12. Furneaux, *William Wilberforce*, 5.

13. Pollock, *Wilberforce*, 5.

14. For a Roman Catholic treatment of the idea of "enthusiasm" see John Knox, *Enthusiasm: A Chapter in the History of Religion* (1950, reprint, Notre Dame, Ind.: Notre Dame Press, 1994).

15. Oliver Warner, *William Wilberforce and His Times* (New York: Arco Publishing Company, 1962), 24.

16. Ibid.

17. Furneaux, *William Wilberforce*, 11.

18. R. G. Collingwood, *The Idea of History* (London: Oxford University Press, 1962), 52.

19. Warner, *Wilberforce and His Times*, 29.

20. Furneaux, *William Wilberforce*, 16.

21. Ibid.

22. Warner, *Wilberforce and His Times*, 29.

23. Pollock, *Wilberforce*, 26.

24. Ibid., 27.

25. Stephen, *Essays*, 212.

26. Pollock, *Wilberforce*, 27.

27. Furneaux, *William Wilberforce*, 30.

28. Pollock, *Wilberforce*, 32.

29. Furneaux, *William Wilberforce*, 32.

30. Ibid., 33.

31. Phillip Doddridge, *The Rise and Progress of Religion in the Soul* (London: T. Hamilton, 1824).

32. Furneaux, *William Wilberforce*, 34.

33. Ibid., 35.

34. Ibid., 36.

35. Ibid.

36. For the entire letter see A. M. Wilberforce, ed., *Private Papers of William Wilberforce* (New York: Burt Franklin, n.d.), 12–15.

37. Ibid.

38. Garth Lean, *God's Politician,* 38.

39. Warner, *Wilberforce and His Times*, 36.

40. Lean, *God's Politician*, 39.

41. Pollock, *Wilberforce*, 38.

42. Lean, *God's Politician*, 42.

43. Patrick Cormack, *Wilberforce: The Nation's Conscience* (London: Pickering & Inglis, 1983), 43.

44. Warner, *Wilberforce and His Times*, 40.

45. Ibid., 41.

46. Furneaux, *William Wilberforce*, 55–56.

47. Ibid., 72.

48. Roger Anstey, *The Atlantic Slave Trade and British Abolition* (New Jersey: Humanities Press, 1975), 255.

49. Coupland, *Wilberforce*, 72; Coupland, *BASM*, 55.

50. Coupland, *BASM*, 22–26.

51. Warner, *Wilberforce and His Times*, 61.

52. Lean, *God's Politician*, 54–55.

53. John Wesley, *The Works of John Wesley,* vol. 13 (1872; reprint, Grand Rapids, Mich.: Baker Book House, 1979), 153.

54. Charles Colson, "William Wilberforce," *Chosen Vessels: Portraits of Ten Outstanding Christian Men*, ed. Charles Turner (Ann Arbor, Mich.: Servant Publications, 1985), 52.

55. Ibid., 53.

56. Ibid.

57. Ibid.

58. Furneaux, *William Wilberforce*, 95.

59. Colson, "William Wilberforce," 56.

60. Ibid., 98.

61. Howse, *Saints in Politicians*, 45.

62. Furneaux, *William Wilberforce*, 137. See also Carl B. Crone, *The English Jacobins: Reformers in Late Eighteenth Century England* (New York: Charles Scribner's Sons, 1968).

63 Robert and Samuel Wilberforce, *Life of Wilberforce*, vol. 2 (London: John Murray, 1838), 399–400.

64. Ibid.

65. Ibid.

66. Furneaux, *William Wilberforce*, 144, 146.

67. Robert and Samuel Wilberforce, *Life of Wilberforce*, 209.

68. Furneaux, *William Wilberforce*, 151–52.

69. Ibid., 161.

70. Ibid., 163.

71. Lean, *God's Politician*, 143.

72. Thomas Paine, *The Age of Reason* in *The Selected Work of Tom Paine* (New York: Modern Library, 1946).

73. Howse, *Saints in Politics*, 53.

74. Ibid., 56–57.

75. Travers Buxton, *William Wilberforce: The Story of a Great Crusade* (London: The Religious Tract Society, n.d.), 94–95.

76. Coupland, *Wilberforce*, 280.

77. Buxton, *Wilberforce: Great Crusade*, 100.

78. Lecky, *History of European Morals*, 153.

79. Furneaux, *William Wilberforce*, 265.

80. Warner, *Wilberforce and His Times*, 112.

81. Cormack, *Wilberforce: Nation's Conscience*, 102.

82. Ibid.

83. Cormack, *Wilberforce: Nation's Conscience*, 103.

84. Furneaux, *William Wilberforce*, 316–18.

85. Ibid., 305.

86. Ibid., 307.

87. Ibid., 363.

88. Lean, *God's Politician*, 168.

89. Warner, *Wilberforce and His Times*, 133.

90. Ibid., 137.

91. Ibid., 135.

92. Ibid.

93. H. M. Wheeler, *The Slave's Champion, or A Sketch of the Life, Deeds, and Historical Days of William Wilberforce* (London: privately printed, 1861), 144–46.
94. Coupland, *Wilberforce*, 392–93.
95. Coupland, *BASM*, 124.
96. Coupland, *Wilberforce*, 396.
97. Ibid., 404.
98. Furneaux, *William Wilberforce*, 422.
99. Ibid., 433–34.
100. Ibid., 432.
101. Ibid., 435.
102. Cormack, *Wilberforce*, 108.
103. Furneaux, *William Wilberforce*, 452.
104. Ibid., 453.
105. Ibid., 454.
106. Ibid.
107. Ibid., 456.

PART II: THE CHARACTER OF WILLIAM WILBERFORCE

1. Gurney in Warner, *Wilberforce and His Times*, 166.
2. Robert Hall in Buxton, *Wilberforce: Great Crusade*, 129.
3. M. Seeley, *The Later Evangelical Fathers* (London: Seeley, Jackson, & Halliday, 1879), 230.
4. A. M. Wilberforce, *Private Papers*, 252.
5. Buxton, *Wilberforce: Great Crusade*, 30.
6. Coupland, *Wilberforce*, 186.
7. Buxton, *Wilberforce: Great Crusade*, 27–28.
8. Ibid., 41.
9. Furneaux, *William Wilberforce*, 83.
10. A. M. Wilberforce, *Private Papers*, 239.
11. Furneaux, *William Wilberforce*, 45.
12. Buxton, *Wilberforce: Great Crusade*, 56.
13. A. M. Wilberforce, *Private Papers*, 191.
14. William Connor Sydney, *England and the English in the Eighteenth Century,* vol. 2 (London: Ward & Downey, 1891), 325.

15. Seeley, *Evangelical Fathers*, 12.
16. Furneaux, *William Wilberforce*, 41.
17. Sydney, *England*, 326.
18. Ibid., 327–28.
19. Furneaux, *William Wilberforce*, 42.
20. S. C. Carpenter, *Church and People, 1789–1889: A History of the Church of England from William Wilberforce to "Lux Mundi"* (New York: The Macmillan Company, 1933), 27.
21. Furneaux, *William Wilberforce*, 41.
22. Carpenter, *Church and People*, 28.
23. Buxton, *Wilberforce: Great Crusade*, 133.
24. A. M. Wilberforce, *Private Papers*, 206.
25. William Wilberforce, *A Practical View of Christianity*, Kevin Charles Belmonte, ed. (1797; reprint, Peabody, Mass.: Hendrickson Publishers, 1996), xxi.
26. Coupland, *Wilberforce*, 199.
27. Ibid.
28. Furneaux, *William Wilberforce*, 146.
29. Buxton, *Wilberforce: Great Crusade*, 56.
30. Pollock, *Wilberforce*, 151–52.
31. Wilberforce in Coupland, *Wilberforce*, 148.
32. Furneaux, *William Wilberforce*, 287.
33. Ibid., 232.
34. Ibid., 406.
35. Buxton, *Wilberforce: Great Crusade*, 149–50.
36. Ibid., 150; Furneaux, *William Wilberforce*, 181–82.
37. A. M. Wilberforce, *Private Papers*, 166, 183.
38. Ibid., 184.
39. Ibid., 201–2.
40. Furneaux, *William Wilberforce*, 11.
41. Ibid., 150.
42. Seeley, *Evangelical Fathers*, 209.
43. Buxton, *Wilberforce: Great Crusade*, 78.
44. A. M. Wilberforce, *Private Papers*, 265.
45. Pollock, *Wilberforce*, 185.
46. Stephen, *Essays*, 222–23.

47. Furneaux, *William Wilberforce*, 274.
48. Ibid., 273–74.
49. Ibid., 275–76.
50. Coupland, *Wilberforce*, 208.
51. Buxton, *Wilberforce: Great Crusade*, 170.
52. Seeley, *Evangelical Fathers*, 207.
53. Buxton, *Wilberforce: Great Crusade*, 169.
54. Stephen, *Essays*, 222.
55. A. M. Wilberforce, *Private Papers*, 250.
56. Pollock, *Wilberforce*, 15.
57. Ibid.
58. Furneaux, *William Wilberforce*, 292.
59. Os Guiness, ed., *Character Counts: Leadership Qualities in Washington, Wilberforce, Lincoln and Solzhenitsyn* (Grand Rapids, Mich.: Baker Book House, 1999), 74–75.
60. Stephen, *Essays*, 221, 225.
61. Furneaux, *William Wilberforce*, 293.
62. Ibid., 254.
63. Ibid., 166.
64. Dorothy Sayers, *Creed or Chaos?* (London: Methuen & Co., 1947), 69.
65. A. M. Wilberforce, *Private Papers*, 202.
66. Proverbs 13:20, author's translation.
67. Furneaux, *William Wilberforce*, 6–7.
68. A. M. Wilberforce, "Sketch of Pitt," in *Private Papers*, 61ff.
69. A. M. Wilberforce, *Private Papers*, 202.
70. Lean, *God's Politician*, 105.
71. Seeley, *Evangelical Fathers*, 226–27.
72. A. M. Wilberforce, *Private Papers*, 202.
73. Lean, *God's Politician*, 112.
74. Bruce Hindmarsh, "Aristocratic Activists," *Christian History* 53 (1997): 24.
75. Ibid., 25–26.
76. Ibid.
77. Furneaux, *William Wilberforce*, 117.
78. Wilberforce, *Practical View*, 259.

79. John Marlowe, *The Puritan Tradition in English Life* (Cresset, 1957), quoted in Lean, *God's Politician*, 74.
80. Ibid.
81. Lean, *God's Politician*, 85.
82. Pollock, *Wilberforce*, 139.
83. Roger Anstey, *The Atlantic Slave Trade and British Abolition*, quoted in Lean, *God's Politician*, 70.
84. Galatians 5:6, author's translation.
85. A. M. Wilberforce, *Private Papers*, 179.
86. Buxton, *Wilberforce: Great Crusade*, 57.
87. Seeley, *Evangelical Fathers*, 211–12.
88. Lean, *God's Politician*, 163.
89. Furneaux, *William Wilberforce*, 378.
90. Wilberforce, *Practical View*, 92.
91. Furneaux, *William Wilberforce*, 287–88.
92. Coupland, *Wilberforce*, 97.
93. Ibid., 112.
94. *Life*, quoted in Coupland, *Wilberforce*, 98.
95. Furneaux, *William Wilberforce*, 287; Coupland, *Wilberforce*, 98.
96. Furneaux, *William Wilberforce*, 208.
97. Wilberforce, *Practical View*, 103.
98. Coupland, *Wilberforce*, 188.
99. Wilberforce, *Practical View*, 104–5.
100. Ibid., 103–4.
101. Ibid.
102. Coupland, *Wilberforce*, 188.
103. Ibid., 190–91.
104. A. M. Wilberforce, *Private Papers*, 221.
105. Coupland, *Wilberforce*, 191.
106. Pollock, *Wilberforce*, 67.
107. Ibid., 65, 66, 68.
108. Ibid., 68–69.
109. Furneaux, *William Wilberforce*, 238.
110. Coupland, *Wilberforce*, 192.
111. Wilberforce in Howse, *Saints in Politics*, 91.
112. Ibid., 65.

113. Ibid.
114. Furneaux, *William Wilberforce,* 120.
115. Ibid.
116. Howse, *Saints in Politics,* 83.
117. Ibid., 88–89.
118. Ibid., 90.
119. Ibid., 91.
120. Ibid., 91–92.
121. Ibid.
122. A. M. Wilberforce, *Private Papers,* 188–89.
123. Coupland, *Wilberforce,* 147.
124. Ibid., 150.
125. Lean, *God's Politician,* 125–26.
126. Coupland, *Wilberforce,* 154.
127. Ibid., 244.
128. Pollock, *Wilberforce,* 193.
129. Wilberforce in Lean, *God's Politician,* 55.
130. Buxton, *Wilberforce: Great Crusade,* 92.
131. Ibid., 65.
132. Coupland, *Wilberforce,* 175.
133. Furneaux, *William Wilberforce,* 260–61.
134. Pollock, *Wilberforce,* 219.
135. Wilberforce, *Practical View,* 247.
136. Quoted in Pollock, *Wilberforce,* 219–20.
137. Wilberforce, *Practical View,* 218.
138. A. M. Wilberforce, *Private Papers,* 180.
139. Coupland, *Wilberforce,* 109.
140. Ibid., 177.
141. Ibid., 177–78.
142. Pollock, *Wilberforce,* 250.
143. Coupland, *Wilberforce,* 379.
144. Lean, *God's Politician,* 93–94.
145. Ibid., 94.
146. Pollock, *Wilberforce,* 287.
147. Ibid.
148. Carpenter, *Church and People,* 46.

149. A. M. Wilberforce, *Private Papers*, 254.
150. Pollock, *Wilberforce*, 78–79.
151. Ibid., 144.
152. Ibid., 178.
153. Ibid., 280.
154. Ibid., 302.
155. A. M. Wilberforce, *Private Papers*, 187.
156. Furneaux, *William Wilberforce*, 82.
157. Ibid., 81.
158. Ibid., 82.
159. Pollock, *Wilberforce*, 80.
160. Ibid., 81.
161. Thomas De Quincey, *The Confessions of an English Opium Eater* (London: J. M. Dent & Co., n.d.). Both De Quincey and Coleridge were opium addicts at certain periods of their lives. De Quincey was taking upward of 1,200 drops of laudanum, or over fifty grams of opium daily.
162. Wilberforce in Buxton, *Wilberforce: Great Crusade*, 139.
163. Warner, *Wilberforce and His Times*, 85.
164. Ibid.
165. Furneaux, *William Wilberforce*, 166.
166. Ibid., 165.
167. Ibid., 170.
168. Ibid., 165.
169. Buxton, *Wilberforce: Great Crusade*, 138–39.
170. Wilberforce in Warner, *Wilberforce and His Times*, 157.
171. Buxton, *Wilberforce: Great Crusade*, 140.
172. Thornton in Pollock, *Wilberforce*, 231.
173. Lean, *God's Politician*, 149.
174. Pollock, *Wilberforce*, 232.
175. Ibid.
176. Lean, *God's Politician*, 149.
177. Ibid., 148.
178. A. M. Wilberforce, *Private Papers*, 176–77.
179. Ibid., 178.
180. Wilberforce in Coupland, *Wilberforce*, 252.

181. Warner, *Wilberforce and His Times*, 20.
182. Ibid.
183. Coupland, *Wilberforce*, 257.
184. Furneaux, *William Wilberforce*, 403.
185. John Locke, *Two Treatises of Civil Government* (1690; reprint, London: Everyman's Library, 1966), bk. 1, ch. 1, sec. 1; bk. 2, ch. 4, sec. 24.
186. Richard Baxter, *A Christian Directory*, Vol. I of *Baxter's Practical Works* (Morgan, Pa: Soli Deo, Gloria Publications, 1996 [1846]), pt. 2, ch. 14.
187. Boswell, *Samuel Johnson*.
188. Anstey, *Atlantic Stave Trade*.
189. John Wesley, "Thoughts Upon Slavery" in *The Works of John Wesley*, 3rd ed., vol. 11 (1872; reprint, Grand Rapids, Mich.: Baker Book House, 1979), 59ff. This tract was originally published in 1774.
190. Pollock, *Wilberforce*, 304.
191. Stephen, *Essays*, 247.
192. Wilberforce in Furneaux, *William Wilberforce*, 195.
193. Ibid., 54.
194. Ibid.
195. Danny Day, "Brutality Behind Bars," *Christian History* 53 (1997): 39.
196. Furneaux, *William Wilberforce*, 379.
197. Lean, *God's Politician*, xxii.
198. Coupland, *Wilberforce*, 47.
199. Ibid., 300.
200. Wilberforce in ibid., 258.
201. Furneaux, *William Wilberforce*, 402.
202. Buxton, *Wilberforce: Great Crusade*, 82.
203. Furneaux, *William Wilberforce*, 106–7.
204. Ibid., 402.
205. Seeley, *Evangelical Fathers*, 227.
206. Furneaux, *William Wilberforce*, 184.
207. Stephen, *Essays*, 260.
208. Trevelyan in Warner, *Wilberforce and His Times*, 166.

209. Wilberforce in Furneaux, *William Wilberforce,* 285–86.
210. Ibid., 12–13.
211. Ibid., 285–86.
212. Ibid., 284.
213. Lean, *God's Politician,* 28.
214. Coupland, *Wilberforce,* 102.
215. Furneaux, *William Wilberforce,* 286.
216. Cormack, *Wilberforce,* 58.
217. Stephen, *Essays,* 269–70.
218. Buxton, *Wilberforce: Great Crusade,* 67.
219. Cormack, *Wilberforce,* 59.
220. J. C. Colquhoun in ibid.
221. Philip Dorner Stanhope, *Letters of Lord Chesterfield* (London: Oxford University Press, 1929), 200.
222. Wilberforce in Furneaux, *William Wilberforce,* 9.
223. Ibid., 273.
224. Cormack, *Wilberforce,* 104.
225. Ibid.
226. Wilberforce, *Practical View,* 107.
227. Ibid., 111.
228. Ibid., 114–15, 117–18.
229. Ibid., 117.
230. Ibid., 112.
231. Ibid., 120.
232. Wilberforce, *Practical View,* 232.
233. Ibid., 125.
234. Ibid., 171.
235. Ibid.
236. Furneaux, *William Wilberforce,* 421.
237. Ibid.
238. Buxton, *Wilberforce: Great Crusade,* 163–64.
239. Coupland, *Wilberforce,* 423.
240. Furneaux, *William Wilberforce,* 454–55.
241. Wilberforce in ibid., 377–78.
242. Cormack, *Wilberforce,* 101.
243. Stephen, *Essays,* 256–57.

244. Colquhoun in Cormack, *Wilberforce*, 103.

245. Furneaux, *William Wilberforce*, 202–3.

246. Ibid., 377.

247. Wilberforce, *Practical View*, 208.

248. Wilberforce in Pollock, *Wilberforce*, 304.

249. Christopher D. Hancock, "The Shrimp Who Stopped Slavery," *Christian History* 53 (1997): 17.

250. Lean, *God's Politician*, 65.

251. Ibid., 64.

252. Warner, *Wilberforce and His Times*, 103.

PART III: THE LEGACY OF WILLIAM WILBERFORCE

1. Buxton, *Wilberforce: Great Crusade*, 43.

2. Seeley, *Evangelical Fathers*, 214–15.

3. Stephen, *Essays*, 246.

4. Furneaux, *William Wilberforce*, 283.

5. q. v.

6. Edmund Burke, *Reflections on the Revolution in France* (1790; reprint, New York: The Liberal Arts Press, 1955).

7. Coupland, *Wilberforce*, 121.

8. Ibid., 221. Evangelicals in general believed in God's temporal judgment on men and nations for sin. See Anstey, *Atlantic Slave Trade*, 157 ff.

9. Coupland, *Wilberforce*, 430.

10. Howse, *Saints in Politics*, 178.

11. Ibid.

12. Ibid., 179.

13. G. M. Trevelyan, *Life of Lord Macaulay,* vol. 1 (London: 1876), I., 62.

14. Colson, "William Wilberforce," 66.

15. Howse, *Saints in Politics*, 183.

16. *Life*, quoted in Coupland, *Wilberforce*, 302–3.

17. Himmelfarb quoted in David J. Vaughan, *The Pillars of Leadership* (Nashville, Tenn.: Cumberland House Publishing, 2000), 39.

18. C. S. Lewis, *The Abolition of Man* (London: Geoffrey Bles, 1962), 21.
19. Coupland, *Wilberforce*, 347.
20. Howse, *Saints in Politics*, viii.

# SELECTED BIBLIOGRAPHY

## Books

Anstey, Roger. *The Atlantic Slave Trade and British Abolition.* Atlantic Highlands, N.J.: Humanities Press, 1975.

Ashton, T. S. *The Industrial Revolution 1760–1830.* 1948. Reprint, London: Oxford University Press, 1955.

Baxter, Richard. *Baxter's Practical Works.* 1846. Reprint, Morgan, Penn.: Soli Deo Gloria Publications, 1996.

Boswell, James. *The Life of Samuel Johnson.* New York: Modern Library, 1932.

Brown, Ford K. *Fathers of the Victorians: The Age of Wilberforce.* Cambridge: University Press, 1961.

Burke, Edmund. *Reflections on the Revolution in France.* 1790. Reprint, New York: The Liberal Arts Press, 1955.

Buxton, Travers. *William Wilberforce: The Story of a Great Crusade.* London: The Religious Tract Society, n.d.

Carpenter, S. C. *Church and People, 1789–1889: A History of the Church of England from William Wilberforce to "Lux Mundi."* New York: The Macmillan Company, 1933.

Churchill, Winston S. *A History of the English-Speaking Peoples.* New York: Dodd, Mead & Company, 1957.

Clarkson, Thomas. *Strictures on a Life of William Wilberforce by the Rev. W. Wilberforce and the Rev. S. Wilberforce.* 1838. Reprint, Freeport, N.Y.: Books for Libraries Press, 1971.

Cone, Carl B. *The English Jacobins: Reformers in Late Eighteenth Century England.* New York: Charles Scribner's Sons, 1968.

Copeland, Lewis, ed. *The World's Greatest Speeches.* New York: The Book League of America, 1942.

Cormack, Patrick. *Wilberforce: The Nation's Conscience.* London: Pickering & Inglis, 1983.

Coupland, Reginald. *Wilberforce.* 1923. Reprint, London: Collins, 1945.

———. *The British Anti-Slavery Movement.* 1933. Reprint, London: Frank Cass & Co., 1964.

Cowie, Leonard W. *William Wilberforce 1759–1833: A Bibliography.* New York: Greenwood Press, 1992.

De Quincey, Thomas. *The Confessions of an English Opium Eater.* London: J. M. Dent & Co., n.d.

Doddridge, Phillip. *The Rise and Progress of Religion in the Soul.* 19th ed. London: T. Hamilton, 1824.

Douglas, J. D., ed. *The New International Dictionary of the Christian Church.* Grand Rapids, Mich.: Zondervan, 1978.

———. *Who's Who in Christian History.* Wheaton, Ill.: Tyndale House Publishers, Inc., 1992.

Dowley, Tim, ed. *A Lion's Handbook: The History of Christianity.* Oxford: Lion Publishing, 1977.

Egstrom, Ted W. *The Making of a Christian Leader.* Grand Rapids, Mich.: Zondervan Publishing House, 1976.

Eltis, David and James Walvin, eds. *The Abolition of the Atlantic Slave Trade: Origins and Effects in Europe, Africa, and the Americas.* Madison, Wis.: The University of Wisconsin Press, 1981.

*Encyclopedia of Religion and Ethics.* 13 vols. 1920. Reprint, New York: Charles Scribner's Sons, 1934.

Everett, Susanne. *History of Slavery.* Edison, N.J.: Chartwell Books, Inc., 1999.

Fladeland, Betty. *Abolitionists and Working-Class Problems in the Age of Industrialization.* Baton Rouge: Louisiana State University Press, 1984.

Furneaux, Robin. *William Wilberforce.* London: Hamish Hamilton, 1974.

Gardiner, Juliet, ed. *History Today: Who's Who in British History.* London: Collins & Brown Limited, 2000.

Guinness, Os. *Character Counts: Leadership Qualities in Washington, Wilberforce, Lincoln and Solzhenitsyn.* Grand Rapids, Mich.: Baker Book House, 1999.

Hall, Robert. *The Works of Robert Hall, M. A.* 2nd ed. London: Holdsworth and Ball, 1833.

Henson, Hervert Hensley. *The Church of England.* Cambridge: Cambridge University Press, 1939.

Howse, Ernest Marshall. *Saints in Politics: The Clapham Sect and the Growth of Freedom.* Toronto: University of Toronto Press, 1952.

Kenyon, J. P., ed. *Dictionary of British History.* New York: Stein and Day, 1983.

Knox, Ronald A. *Enthusiasm: A Chapter in the History of Religion.* 1950. Reprint, Notre Dame, Ind.: University of Notre Dame Press, 1994.

Kramnick, Isaac, ed. *The Portable Enlightenment Reader.* New York: Penguin Books, 1995.

Lean, Garth. *God's Politician: William Wilberforce's Struggle.* Colorado Springs: Helmers & Howard, 1987.

Lecky, William Edward Hartpole. *History of European Morals.* 1869. Reprint, New York: George Braziller, 1955.

———. *Democracy and Liberty.* New York: Longmans, Green and Co., 1896.

Lewis, C. S. *The Abolition of Man.* London: Geoffrey Bles, 1962.

Lindsay, J. O., ed. *The New Cambridge Modern History, Vol. VII. The Old Regime 1713–63.* Cambridge: Cambridge University Press, 1957.

Locke, John. *Two Treatises of Civil Government.* London: Everyman's Library, 1966.

Macaulay, Thomas Babington. *Critical, Historical, and Miscellaneous Essays and Poems.* New York: The Publishers Plate Renting Company, n.d.

Magill, Frank N., ed. *Great Events: Modern European Series II, 1801–1899.* Englewood Cliffs, N.J.: Salem Press, 1973.

More, Hannah. *Practical Piety: or, The Influence of the Religion of the Heart on the Conduct of Life.* Philadelphia: American Sunday-School Union, n.d.

Morgan, Kenneth O., ed. *The Oxford History of Britain.* Revised edition. New York: Oxford University Press, 1999.

Paine, Thomas and Howard Fast. *The Selected Work of Tom Paine.* New York: Modern Library, 1946.

Pollack, John Charles. *Wilberforce.* New York: St. Martin's Press, 1977.

Richardson, A. E. *Georgian England: A Survey of Social Life, Trades, Industries & Art from 1700 to 1820.* London: B. T. Batsford, 1931.

Routh, C. R. W., ed. *Who's Who in History, Vol. II. England.* Oxford: Blackwell, 1964.

Seeley, M. *The Later Evangelical Fathers: John Thornton, John Newton, William Cowper, Thomas Scott, Richard Cecil, William Wilberforce, Charles Simeon, Henry Martyn, Josiah Pratt.* London: Seeley, Jackson & Halliday, 1879.

Sheldon, Henry C. *History of the Christian Church.* 1895. Reprinted, Pennsylvania: Hendrickson Publishers, Inc., 1994.

Sherrard, O. A. *Freedom From Fear: The Slave and His Emancipation.* New York: St. Martin's Press, 1961.

Stanhope, Philip Dormer (Lord Chesterfield). *Letters of Lord Chesterfield.* London: Oxford University Press, 1929.

Stephen, James. *Essays in Ecclesiastical Biography.* London: Longman, Brown, Green, and Longmans, 1850.

Stephen, Leslie and Sidney Lee, eds. *Dictionary of National Biography, Vol. XXI.* 1917. Reprint, Oxford: Oxford University Press, 1959–69.

Sydney, William Connor. *England and the English in the Eighteenth Century.* London: Ward & Downey, 1891.

Trevelyan, G. M. *History of England.* 1926. Reprinted, Garden City, N.Y.: Doubleday & Company, Inc., 1953.

Troeltsch, Ernst. *The Social Teaching of the Christian Churches.* New York: The Macmillan Company, 1931.

Turner, Charles. *Chosen Vessels: Portraits of Ten Outstanding Christian Men.* Ann Arbor, Mich.: Servant Publications, 1985.

Vaughan, David J. *The Pillars of Leadership.* Nashville, Tenn.: Cumberland House Publishing, 2000.

Viault, Birdsall S. *English History.* New York: McGraw-Hill, 1992.

Warner, Oliver. *William Wilberforce and His Times.* New York: Arco Publishing Company, 1962.

Wesley, John. *The Works of John Wesley.* 3rd ed. 1872. Reprint, Grand Rapids, Mich.: Baker Book House, 1979.

Wheeler, H. M. *The Slave's Champion, or A Sketch of the Life, Deeds, and Historical Days of William Wilberforce.* London: privately printed, 1861.

Wilberforce, A. M., ed. *Private Papers of William Wilberforce.* New York: Burt Franklin, [1897].

Wilberforce, Robert and Samuel. *Life of Wilberforce.* London: John Murray, 1838.

Wilberforce, William. *A Practical View of Christianity.* Edited by Kenneth Charles Belmonte. Peabody, Mass.: Hendrikson Publishers, 1996.

_____. *A Practical View of the Prevailing Religious System of Professed Christians, in the Higher and Middle Classes, Contrasted with Real Christianity.* New York: American Tract Society, n.d.

## Magazines & Journals

Colson, Charles W. "Standing Tough Against All Odds," *Christianity Today* (September 6, 1985): 26–33.

Day, Danny. "Brutality Behind Bars," *Church History* 53 (1997): 39.

Hancock, Christopher D. "The Shrimp Who Stopped Slavery," *Church History* 53 (1997): 17.

Hindmarsh, Bruce. "Aristocratic Activists," *Church History* 53 (1997): 24.

Schlossberg, Herbert. "How Great Awakenings Happen," *First Things* 106 (October 2000): 46–51.

# INDEX

Printed in the USA
CPSIA information can be obtained
at www.ICGtesting.com
JSHW082150140824
68134JS00014B/168

9 781620 453926